SID'S STORY:

A Father-Daughter Journey

By

Karen Vogel (and Sid Vogel)

Cecily —
Thank you for inspiring
so many people, including
me! And for the work
you do every day... Have a
pickle for Sid.
Hugs,
Karen

Contents

Foreword

Fermentation

My father Sidney loved pickles more than anything, aside from his family. His obsession probably started as a child, walking the streets of Brooklyn. The briny barrels promised a cheap and tasty treat during the hard times of the Depression. Fast forward to his final days, almost 96 years old, when all he wanted was a half sour dill with a satisfying crunch. He was a simple yet complex man, and always enjoyed a good Jewish joke.

For those not familiar with the historical significance of pickles from the Lower East Side of New York, "real" pickles are barrel-cured cucumbers. The pickles saturate in salt brine with garlic and spices. Then the pickles are stored in wooden oak barrels, up to six months. The pickle business has evolved from street vendors with push carts, to local neighborhood stores, to large manufacturing factories.

This is a story of a delightful friendship between my Dad and me, a surprise for both of us, in the last decade of his life. Nine years ago I starting writing a blog, titled "Aging Quirky," for comic relief when my mother and father became high maintenance elderly people. Before that phase they were just parents, smart and funny and sometimes annoying. I experienced unconditional love and chafed from supervision. They made sure I became an educated, confident and politically liberal woman. I appreciated their support and found my own path after college, checking in to report milestones. Much to my surprise (and ambivalence), after my father's retirement they followed me to Southern California in 1982 while I was in graduate school. I kept moving up the West Coast, landing in Seattle in 1994, where I still live. They stayed in San Diego and bemoaned the lack of decent bagels. I visited them once a year and called them once a week, dutiful as always.

Realizing your folks have embarrassing eccentricities is hard enough during adolescence. As a middle-aged person, discovering your parents need help to get through the day is shocking. How did that happen? Guilt, anxiety and obligation colored every conversation. In 2008 my mother Doris started experiencing a significant health decline; my father eventually became a full time caregiver. What he also undertook, unknown to me and my brother Dan, was writing his autobiography beginning in 1995, at age 73. He eventually shared his writings with us and continued writing updates until shortly before he died in July 2018.

Sid's story, along with my blog posts, highlights the challenges of aging from two perspectives – father and daughter - intertwined yet unique experiences. However, this is primarily his story, with my well-intentioned editing, to honor his memory and life history.

Chapter 1

Sid the Writer

When things are challenging, it's useful to have a sense of humor. Here's how my father titled his personal journal in September 1995:

> MY LIFE: An Autobiography by Sidney Vogel.
> Born: September 2, 1922. Died: (Not Yet).

Little did Dad know he would have another 23 years to document his adventures.

In 1995, Sid started documenting his thoughts on a typewriter, then a desktop computer, one peck at a time, late at night. It was his private time while Doris was sleeping. A tech nerd at heart, he was proud to have patched together a personal computer with recycled parts. He taught himself how to use AOL, but only surfed the internet sporadically due to the restraints of a dial-up phone modem. It didn't make sense to spend money to get a faster connection. He liked the slowness.

> "Here I am, at age 73, staring at a blank monitor screen, wondering how to begin. My children and my grandson never really knew me as a person. I was the provider who left early in the morning and returned in the evening five days a week. On weekends and holidays, there were chores to be done and grounds to be maintained and little time to spend with the children. This is to be my legacy to them of their roots in my life experiences. Thinking back, I had an interesting life with many odd experiences. It was a time frame that has been a total blank in their knowledge."

Sid had been using a program called Framework, an early version of word processing. The software kept crashing, there was no user support and it finally corrupted into oblivion. In March 2000 he realized a different strategy was needed. While I was visiting he handed over a binder of 29 single-spaced pages and sheepishly asked "Can you help?"

Although I'd heard snippets over the decades, I read the full story that night. Dad's diligence wasn't a surprise; however asking for assistance was new. I talked with my brother, a computer training consultant. While learning more about family history would be fun, what mostly needed preservation was Dad's self-esteem regarding his technical ability.

We found an optical scanning recognition program to convert the document into Word. Initial typos were amusing, starting with the title: "My Life" became "Mr. Lies." A reference to the "Atomic Bomb" was converted to "Atari Boob". The phrase "an error had been made in the code" was changed to "an error had been made nude." Oh well. I painstakingly corrected each glitch while Dad got excited about how to navigate Windows. Late night students, both of us.

Chapter 2

Childhood

Sid:

I was born in the back bedroom of a third floor flat at 9 DeKalb Ave, in an old law tenement in Brooklyn. I was the fifth child and son of Daniel David Vogel and Annie Vogel (nee Mandel). Dave, as he was called, had emigrated from South Africa about 1903. Annie had emigrated from Poland about 1905. They met as teenagers and got married in 1910. Their first child was Henrietta, in 1912, followed by Ruth in 1914, then Harold in 1917, Stanley in 1920, and then I came along in 1922. We lived in a square building with rooms running from one end to the other like the cars of a railroad train, hence the name of railroad flats. We were fortunate to live in a building with an individual toilet for each apartment. Many of the buildings had a shared toilet per floor.

There was a massive coal stove in the kitchen and a sink with running cold water. Hot water was made in large pots heated on the coal stove. The weekly bath was a contrivance brought into the kitchen and partially filled with hot water from the stove. The girls got their baths separately with the boys excluded from the kitchen. The same water was used for all three boys. As the youngest, I was last in line. The same rule applied to clothing. I wore the hand-me-downs from the older boys. The neighborhood was a polyglot mix of immigrants from middle and southern Europe and black migrants from Southern states.

A trolley line ran through DeKalb Avenue. Local streets were named for heroes of the Revolutionary War. Our favorite game was punchball which involved bouncing a tennis ball on the pavement and hitting it with a closed fist on the rise. The distance which the ball covered was measured in "sewers" which were marked by cast iron sewer covers placed in the thoroughfare. I wasn't a good punchball player and an even worse stickball player. I couldn't seem to hit the ball squarely. It didn't seem significant at the time but that peculiarity made a very significant impact upon my adult life.

Elementary school was Public School (P.S.) 25, an old dilapidated building with an outbuilding containing the toilets. The teachers were predominantly Irish and stern disciplinarians. I started to write with my left hand and was struck many times with a hard wooden ruler to correct my deviation from the strict rules. Thus, I was forced to write with my right hand and became ambidextrous, another peculiarity which became very significant in my adult life. Since I wasn't often chosen in making up the ball teams, I spent most of my time reading and rigorously doing all my homework assignments. I found school to be enjoyable and had no trouble maintaining top grades.

When I was seven years old, central heating was installed in the apartment building, which meant a steam pipe in the kitchen and a steam heated radiator in each bedroom. It was sheer luxury in the cold winters to feel warm at home. In the hot summers, blankets were spread on the outside fire escape landing or were dragged up to the flat tarred roof, where we could sleep in the open air. The Big Depression hit in 1929, but was not really felt until the early 1930s. The advantage of being poor: we never noticed the difference in our daily living, except that food was cheaper. I could buy a quart of milk for seven cents.

By 1933, landlords were giving various concessions to lure tenants into their empty apartments. My mother negotiated a ground floor apartment in a much nicer building four blocks away with no rent charge for the first three months. The address was 763 Greene Avenue. I lived there until I got married. She had developed arthritic knees and the three-floor walkup on DeKalb Avenue was too difficult for her. The new address had a central courtyard and every room had a window. There was a gas range and an old fashioned icebox in the kitchen. In 1935 the landlord installed an electric refrigerator. It was a noisy unit with a chattering motor driving the compressor with a connecting belt, but it meant not having to buy a block of ice every other day. We were living in the lap of luxury.

In those days, the school system maintained three tracking levels, slow, average and advanced. As part of the advanced group, I was sent to Mark Hopkins Junior High School, which advanced a year into the first year of high school. The school was a very old structure on Ellery Street in Brooklyn, but the teachers were excellent. It was there I had my first exposure to science and higher levels of mathematics. It was there I was robbed of my lunch box and lunch money. It was also where some weird Italian boy started pummeling me while mumbling something about "Christ killer." I hadn't the faintest idea what he was talking about. Still, I graduated with excellent grades.

Karen's comment:

Law tenements were created by the New York State Tenement House Act of 1901 to ban the construction of dark, poorly ventilated tenement buildings. The law required windows in every room, proper ventilation systems, indoor toilets and fire safeguards. Brooklyn is a very different place these days. Always a small geographic space with a large diverse population, the area has changed from primarily Jewish to Chinese to African American to Irish to Russian to Pakistani heritage.

Now gentrified, Brooklyn has become a trendy place for millennials and artists to set up live/work spaces after being priced out of the high rents of Manhattan. I walked across the Brooklyn Bridge a few years ago for the first time, admiring the beautiful views and architecture. It's hard to visualize a town of poor immigrants from decades ago. There are now many cute stores selling fashionable shirts, and no more pickle barrels on the streets.

Chapter 3

A Boy From Brooklyn

Sid:

Graduates of Mark Hopkins Junior High School could choose from several high schools for their continuing education. I had a difficult decision to make. The most attractive school was Bushwick High School, a coeducational institution with a good academic record. However, my eldest brother, Harold, had achieved about every honor imaginable in his stay at that school. I knew I never could measure up to his record. I wanted to stand on my own ability and make my own mark. I selected Boys High School, an all-male institution within walking distance of home. Boys High also had a very high standard, but I would have no social development during my teen years. It was a handicap that bothered me; I had very few friends and no interaction with girls at all.

I graduated with honors. However, the competition from other Jewish boys was so fierce that I was only seventh in the graduating class and missed out on a state scholarship by one point. I recall the top three boys became distinguished teachers and scholars. Still, my name was engraved on a brass plaque for the Scholastic Hall of Fame.

I graduated Boys High in February 1939. My record was good enough to qualify me for admission to CCNY (City College of New York), a tuition-free municipal college with very high standards. There were two branches to the college, a business School located in downtown Manhattan, and an engineering school way up in the end of the city. Since the business school was an easy subway ride from

Brooklyn, I decided to major in accounting at the downtown branch. I did day sessions and completed my second term in February 1940.

By this time, my father was showing signs of chronic illness. The diagnosis was Hodgkin's disease, a cancer of the lymph glands. He had been working as a driver of a newspaper delivery truck but became too weak to drive a vehicle. The union arranged to get him a job as a foot route to hand deliver bundles of newspapers to individual newsstands. When he got too weak, I sat him in a chair and took over delivery of the papers. Of course, college was out of the question by now. Eventually, he became homebound and I had to get a job of my own. My father died of cancer in January 1942, after 30 months of wasting away. He weighed 85 pounds when he died.

Karen's comment:

Throughout his adulthood, Sid was on the hunt for salty, greasy fast food. During his last 2 weeks of life he was unable to eat or swallow properly, due to a stroke. Not being able to eat solid food was frustrating. His advance directive requests (and common sense) ruled out a feeding tube. Taking pills became impossible without choking. Subsisting on protein milkshakes, even chocolate ones, wasn't a long term option. He dropped weight and became frail, startling since he had always prided himself on his powerful legs and upper body strength.

Palliative care, then hospice, helped make him as comfortable as possible, mostly by stopping all the medications that no longer made sense. While Dad's fast decline was shocking, I hope his last days were not as traumatic as what he had to experience with his own father. He was able to have strawberry ice cream, his favorite flavor; that was his last meal and I fed it to him.

Chapter 4

Finding a Job

Sid:

This was the family situation facing me in 1940. The two girls were married and were struggling with their own problems. My eldest brother, Harold, joined the army in 1937 and was stationed somewhere in Illinois. My other brother, Stanley, had been arrested for petty thievery and was in prison. My father was receiving an allowance from his union and only union members could be drivers. The card could be passed from father to son. I could take my father's card because of his disability and become a truck driver. The other choice was to get a job on my own and save the card as a promise of employment for Stanley when he would finish his jail sentence. I had no desire to become a truck driver and decided to hold the union card prospect for my brother. This was my entrance into the real world.

In the early winter, 1 went to an employment agency in Manhattan and filled out one of the application cards. One of the lines on the card asked for religion. I entered "H" (for Hebrew) and submitted the card to the interviewer. He looked at the card, tore it up and told me to get out of the office because they didn't handle my type. I didn't quite understand and asked for clarification. He said point blank "We don't deal with Jews because they are pushy and trouble makers." I was told to go to the New York State Employment Service office because they were not permitted to discriminate by religion. I went to the state agency. The only open job was a delivery boy for a photoengraving outfit, at the minimum wage of twenty-five cents an hour. Thus began my employment career with the Boro Engraving Company on Willoughby Street in downtown Brooklyn, across the street from the Star Burlesque Theater. By the summer of 1940, I had been promoted to shipping clerk with an increase of ten cents an hour. For working five and a half days a week I was earning a little more than fifteen dollars a week.

My mother had three sisters living in the New York area. Her youngest sister, Sadie, had married Freddie Schunk, a wonderful man who was (gasp) not Jewish. Freddie was a foreman in the installation division of the Western Electric Company, which constructed and modified telephone central offices all over the country for the Bell System. Freddie told me to apply for a job with Western Electric but it would be tricky because they also didn't hire Jews. He briefed me on the Lutheran Church and the answers I should give on certain questions that would be thrown at me to weed out any possible Jews. I applied for a job in the spring of 1941, passing the interview but failing the physical exam.

The exam documented a condition known as varicocele, a testicle hang much lower than the other one. Western Electric would not hire me until I had the surgery to correct the condition. Since we had no money and health insurance was unknown at that time, I was admitted to the Brooklyn Jewish Hospital as a charity case at one of the lecture procedures for the medical school. I was given a spinal injection to block the pain but was wide awake during the operation. The doctor had a throat microphone and would answer questions from the medical students who were viewing the procedure from the surrounding amphitheater. There were more questions from the students than anticipated. As the anesthesia started to wear off, I began to complain about the pain and the nurse told me to keep quiet while the doctor was lecturing. They finally gave me a massive dose of morphine to keep me quiet and I was out for 24 hours.

15

My recuperation took more than a month. Then I had to wait until Western Electric was hiring. Finally, in August 1941, Freddie informed me they were hiring installers again. This was my chance to get on the payroll.

Karen's comment:

Antisemitism was rampant in the 1940s; it was common for employers to pry into medical histories as well as religious beliefs. That kind of intrusion is now illegal. However it would be naïve to believe ethnic, racial, or gender bias is no longer a factor in hiring decisions. It's just more subtle. While health care wasn't nearly as expensive as it is now, payment was a struggle. There were no public assistance programs for another 20 years. Medicare, for Americans 65 years of age or older, wasn't available until 1966. Sid's experience seems bizarre in the modern era of ethics committees and clinical trial protocols. But, it was a practical solution at the time, providing him the freedom he needed.

Chapter 5

Sid's Perspective on Health Care

Fast forward to when I interviewed my father in May 2014; he was 91. The interview was a homework assignment during my training as a patient advocate; I was curious how he would share his thoughts in a more structured format. We sat on a bench above Moonlight Beach near his retirement facility in Encinitas CA. We went to the beach every month during my visits. He loved to watch young people play volleyball, and especially enjoyed the ones wearing bikinis.

Karen: You were born in 1922, when many babies were delivered at home by midwives. Tell me about health care when you were a boy growing up in Brooklyn. How did people get services? How were the services paid for?

Sid: You called the doctor only when near death. People used home remedies; some worked and some didn't. There were no clinics. The family doctor was only called for emergencies. I was actually delivered by a doctor, it cost $5. My father only made $10/week, he had to borrow the money. All of the childhood diseases were rampant. It was customary to have measles, mumps and scarlet fever. Classrooms were crowded and bathrooms were more like a cubicle in the yard. We all grew up on remedies from Europe. The treatment for a cold was a mustard plaster on the chest. I received primitive health care up through 10 years old. I had bad acne as a teenager, the treatment was brewer's yeast (swallowed) – it didn't work. There was also low frequency x-ray treatment to dry up lesions.

Health care was poor during the depression, there was no money. Diphtheria and polio were very prevalent. There were lotions and herbs, black salve. Some people had their blood drawn out of their bodies with cupping, similar to acupuncture today. Women had as many babies as possible, because children died so often. My mother had two miscarriages before she had five children who lived.

Karen: Health insurance wasn't widely available until the 1960s. How did people react to having insurance? What changed?
Sid: Major employers started providing minimal coverage in the 1950s. There were pay deductions, then it became part of union contracts, then it broadened. When you and your brother were born, the company paid for the hospital and pediatric bills. Doctors formed corporations and health care became a business. Appointments rarely exceeded 15 minutes.

Karen: You worked for Western Electric for 40 years. How would you rate the coverage provided by your employer?
Sid: Up until the end of my career the coverage was good. When the phone company mergers happened (the breakup of AT&T and the absorption of Western Electric in 1989) and management changed, the executives received golden parachutes. Coverage was cut back for everyone who remained. Death insurance was cancelled first. I had retiree benefits for decades until I went onto a series of Medicare Health Maintenance Organization (HMO) plans. The first time I had traditional Medicare was this year.

Karen: Health care is complex and fragmented. What has been the most challenging part for you and your family?
Sid: Delays in appointments and treatment. Doctors were loaded with patients and had limited time. Specialists never had time to see anybody. Expertise was fragmented, and many doctors didn't keep up with the latest advances in treatment and research. Doctors tried to give adequate treatment with limited resources. I can't blame the doctors in managed care plans. Secretaries and administrative clerks were dictating how much care patients could get, based on

tables. There was always an appeals process, but I had no occasion to appeal.

Karen: How is your health care experience different in your geriatric years?
Sid: I had to change HMOs several times with a loss of services each time, I had to hunt around. At about age 70-75, we (mostly your mother) started to need more care, with more specialists.

Karen: What is most important to you when selecting a doctor? When you ask questions of your doctors, how do they respond?
Sid: Most of my doctors responded well to my questions. My technical background as an engineer was respected. My issues were high blood pressure, diabetes and heart problems (atrial fibrillation). Not all doctors were respectful and some didn't want to discuss my problems. My current doctor, who you helped me to select, is very good at listening. The doctors were technically the same, personal concern made the difference.

Karen: How would you restructure the health care system if you could advise decision makers?
Sid: Create a single payer, government-sponsored system like Britain, France and Germany. No private corporations, no investors, no highly paid executives. Medicare, as one example of this model, has low overhead and does the job well.

Karen: Health care and prescription drug costs keep rising. In your opinion, what is the biggest cost driver?
Sid: More and more people are getting older, with more needs. The costs of medications are going up. For instance, for my insulin pens, my out-of-pocket allowance went from $30 a year ago to $60 now.

Karen: You've lived into your 90s. Think about your lifestyle. What did you do right? In hindsight, what would you have done differently?

Sid: I violated all of the standard rules for diet. I liked meat, although I tried to balance it with vegetables. Some genetic influence must have helped. I was very active. I liked to walk until spine inflammation became a problem. I didn't smoke or drink – all the people I knew who did are gone. My father was a smoker and he died at age 58. My brother was a heavy smoker who died at age 64.

Karen: Any other comments or insights you want to share?

Sid: Every effort should be made to have health care available in a minimum amount of time – treat minor ailments before they become major ones. Personal budgets should include the costs of health care, just like planning to pay for rent or food. It should be the same mentality about paying for health care. If people look for minimal cost, they will get minimal care. People have no cash reserves. I was fortunate I had savings which were invested wisely. Regarding "Obamacare" insurance reform (America's Affordable Care Act, enacted in 2010), the intent to cover the full population was good. However, insurance programs rely on a huge base of healthy as well as ill people. Younger people need to enroll. They don't expect to get sick and are resistant, they don't see the value. I wouldn't be here today unless my employer-paid pension plan was established when I was young. They tried to cancel the plan later on and weren't successful. I'm sure they hate my guts that I'm still alive!

Karen's comment:

Measles, mumps, scarlet fever, diphtheria and polio have mostly been eradicated by vaccines introduced in the 1950s and 60s. Contagious diseases were greatly feared in Sid's generation, especially the effects of polio. I remember standing in a queue in 1963 for pink sugar cubes soaked with polio vaccine, it tasted so good I tried to go back for seconds. Without childhood vaccines, infectious diseases return due to lack of herd immunity (mass protection when a large percentage of a population has become immune).

Sid became a Type II diabetic at age 50 and depended on daily insulin. Through the next decades he was horrified by the drug's skyrocketing costs, even with insurance. For perspective, when insulin was first developed in 1921, the year before Sid was born, it cost pennies. Now it can cost about $500/month, a price many people can't afford. Lantus, the drug he last used, was $35 per vial when introduced in 2001; in May 2019 the lowest price in my town was $287. Based on family genetics, I may become diabetic at some point. When I need insulin I'll probably be purchasing it in Canada.

Chapter 6

Off to Work

Sid:

One of the tests I had to pass at Western Electric was to identify the colors on the insulation of wires in a telephone cable. Fortunately, Freddie had drilled me in the color sequence used to get around another one of my physical problems, red-green color blindness. I was hired as an installer at forty-five cents an hour for a 44-hour week. My first day at work was a disaster. I reported to the telephone exchange at Avenue R in Brooklyn where modification work was being done.

The old equipment frames were painted a dull black. I was given a gallon of aluminum paint and a brush and was instructed to paint the frames with aluminum paint. I did so with vigor and was quite pleased with my work until one of the technicians came by and recoiled in horror. Nobody had told me all the equipment had functional designations in red on the black framework. I was supposed to copy down the identification data before painting. I had to spend the rest of the day looking up the stencil lettering on a pile of drawings, which I really did not understand.

About two months after I was hired, I was given an out-of-town assignment to work at an installation near the New Jersey border. The job was called a K Carrier installation, which was one of the early attempts to carry multiple voice messages on a single pair of wires. The K system was to carry twelve voice channels. Special low-loss twisted pair wires had been designed. The wires had an outer cloth braid and an inner copper shield protecting the wires with special insulation. When the wires were exposed for connection, they had to be protected to prevent deterioration. I was assigned a job to strip the protective shields from a batch of cables and dip the exposed wires into a tube of synthetic rubber cement.

Nobody told me each cable had a distinctive ribbed pattern on one of the wires; this identity had to be maintained before dipping. After being coated with the cement, all the wires looked alike. When I was ready to connect them, the drawing showed specific connections for the ribbed and smooth insulated wires but they were not identified as such and I wasn't aware of the difference. I dutifully connected all the wires and was quite proud of the neat and professional appearance.

Of course, during the system test, there was a very high noise and interference level. Bell Laboratories engineers had a devil of a time finding the cause. When they finally tracked down my helter-skelter wiring, I pointed out I had never been properly trained. Still, I learned a great deal about the technology of carrier telephony on that job.

After returning home from the carrier job, I became a cable runner. The cables were thick and heavy and I had to crawl across the top of the frames dragging the cables behind me. The cables then had to have the insulation jacket removed and the wires exposed for soldering to connecting terminals. This work was dirty and tiring and I was glad to later be assigned to train as a powerman. Power work specialized in large motors and generators and maintaining large storage battery rooms. It sounded very attractive until I learned more about the tasks.

Powermen prepare heavy steel support bars bolted to ceiling anchors and support frameworks from above. I was handed a dozen hack saw blades and a cutting list for steel support bars which were two inches wide and a half inch thick. In those days, all cutting was with a manual hacksaw. I was led to a basement room containing a load of twelve feet long and was told not to appear on the main floor until all the bars had been cut to specifications. The job took several days and my arms ached for days afterward. Fortunately, I was reassigned to motors and generators; that work was easier and much more fascinating.

One of my fondest memories is working on an engine very few people have ever seen, the one cylinder BOOS illuminating gas engine. Every telephone exchange had generators fed by commercial power to keep the storage batteries charged. The office equipment was actually powered by the batteries themselves. All buildings were provided with an emergency power plant that would take over when commercial power failed for some reason. Most of the newer exchanges had diesel engines for this purpose. The very old exchange on Bushwick Avenue in Brooklyn had the last remaining BOOS engine for emergency power. It was an impressive site, two stories high with a single cylinder three feet in diameter. The shaft was connected to a flywheel twelve feet in diameter and three feet across. The flywheel had two-inch holes drilled into the periphery of the wheel. A long leather belt stretched from the flywheel all across the room to a generator at the other end.

To start the engine, the gas valve would be opened and a manual magneto would be spun to ignite the gas. A quarter inch water line was connected to the cylinder to keep the head from blowing off when the gas was exploded. Before the blast, a long steel rod would be placed into one of the upper holes of the flywheel and three men would hang from the rod to help the flywheel turn for the cycle. At the same time, a "belt dancer" would hop onto the belt and jump up and down to relieve the friction on the belt and get the flywheel turning.

It is difficult to describe the sight of the flywheel turning slowly with three men hanging from the rod and the belt dancer doing his jig on the belt. As soon as the flywheel completed one-half turn, the hanging men jumped down while removing the rod and the dancer would carefully jump off the belt. These precautions were necessary to get the engine going. Each cylinder blast shook the building and the slightly leaky exhaust system filled the room with a burned odor.

The installer's job was to remove the cylinder head and clean the piston cylinder from carbon deposits. The tools involved were immense. The cylinder bolts were three inches across, the removal wrench was six feet long. It took two or three men to loosen the bolts. The engine was retired after the war and replaced with a modern automatic diesel engine.

One of the most unpleasant jobs I faced as a powerman was a simple assignment to clean the muffler for one of the emergency power engines in the Utica Avenue exchange in Brooklyn. I had no idea what the job entailed. The power plant was a four-cylinder Buffalo gas engine. The exhaust led to a muffler hung from the ceiling, eight feet long and three feet across. There was a cover plate on each end with a series of rods extending through the body of the muffler. An array of disks was hung from the rods inside the muffler to absorb the noise. The job assignment: remove the end cover plate, slide out the muffler plates and clean away the carbon deposits. My equipment was a pair of goggles, a chipping hammer and a pail.

After great difficulty removing the cover, I proceeded to do the required cleaning. When I emerged, the rest of the crew howled in laughter. All that was visible on me were eyeballs and teeth. Everything else was jet black. When I came home that evening, my mother wouldn't let me in the house until I had discarded the soot-filled clothes and took a scrubbing bath. It took a long time for the carbon black to get out of my skin crevices. However, this job was a rare exception to the work that usually was enjoyable.

Karen's comment:

In simple terms, a flywheel uses energy input to create spinning mass. When power fluctuates, momentum allows a rotor to continue spinning; the resulting kinetic energy is converted to electricity.

It's hard to imagine all the twists and turns Sid went through with his early jobs, literally and figuratively. He used his wits, smarts and charm to become a skilled telecommunications expert. Later in his career he brought home his work and had my mother correct any color mismatches at night before sneaking the adjustments back the next morning. His red-green color blindness was cause for many family jokes. My mother attempted to lay out his shirts and pants before social events so that he didn't show up in a palette of color clashes.

I can't look at a telephone without appreciating the fascinating history behind its development. Sid even taught me how to wire wall phone jacks. I couldn't get him to use a smartphone - he preferred land lines with coiled cords. However, he took pride in knowing his role helping to build the phone industry. He often commented he was born decades too soon. He would have enjoyed being a coder or programmer at a high tech company.

For a fascinating history of the Western Electric company, manufacturing arm of the Bell Telephone System, read *The Story of Western Electric*[1] (portrayed in a rosy light by the company's public relations department) or *Manufacturing the Future: A History of Western Electric*[2] (a little more dry). In my home town of Seattle, *The Connections Museum*[3] goes back in time with a tour featuring working panel and crossbar electromechanical central-office switches, as well as antique telephones and switchboards. It's way more exciting than it sounds.

[1] www.westernelectric.com/static/library/corporate-history/western-electric-the-story-of-western-electric.pdf

[2] www.amazon.com/Manufacturing-Future-History-Western-Electric/dp/0521651182

[3] www.telcomhistory.org/connections-museum-seattle

Chapter 7

Off to War

Sid:

World War II began in 1939. After Pearl Harbor was bombed and the U.S. entered the war, installation work gradually came to a halt. Those jobs with equipment on hand were allowed to be completed but no new jobs could be started. I was assigned to a team installing air raid alarm systems along the Eastern seaboard. We worked in Connecticut and Massachusetts and lived in low cost rooming houses. That work lasted through the summer and autumn of 1942. After I returned to home base to help finish a job in Brooklyn, I was called into the office by the job supervisor and was told orders had been given to start laying off all installers with less than two years of service. Those with longer service would be taken into the manufacturing operation at Hudson Street in Manhattan, which was making vacuum tubes for the military.

The saving gesture by the company was an offer to pay the difference between military pay and my wage scale for three months and save my job until the war was over - if I would enlist in one of the armed forces. As it happened, I had a military deferment as the sole remaining son supporting a widowed mother. My father had died. My eldest brother, Harold, had joined the Army Air Corps and been reported as missing in action. My other brother, Stanley, had been given the choice of joining the army or serving another prison term. He chose the military option and was with an infantry outfit that had landed in Italy.

I chose to waive my deferment and requested immediate induction into the army. I went down to the local draft board and made this unusual request while surrounded by a roomful of men begging for deferments. They were so taken aback by my patriotic sacrifice that my induction notice appointed me an acting corporal to supervise a load of draftees going to the Grand Central Palace in Manhattan for physical examinations. This hefty responsibility consisted of getting them onto a subway train and getting them off at the right station.

My physical was going along well until the eye examination. I could barely make out the chart with my left eye. The doctor assumed I was faking it to get a deferment but I pointed out I had given up my deferment to join the army. After completing the physical, I was pushed into a room which had a sign "U.S. Navy." I didn't know the Navy had started taking draftees. Fortunately, the Navy officer looked at my physical exam record and rejected me because of defective vision.

I was then sent to the next room which was marked "U.S. Army." An Army major looked at my record and was also considering rejecting me. However the war wasn't going well that day and he felt the army could use every warm body. He told me I would be accepted into the army with the notation "Limited Service" on my induction papers. This meant I would serve only in the continental states and would not be sent overseas. It sounded all right to me; I signed up for the Army.

I received my formal induction notice with instructions to report to Camp Upton in Yaphank, Long Island, in early February 1943. There were special trains on the Long Island Railroad bringing draftees to Camp Upton. I was assigned to a barracks with forty other men and awaited assignment. With my telephone background, I was sure I would be sent to one of the Signal Corps training centers in Fort Monmouth, New Jersey or Camp Crowder in Missouri. Two weeks went by and there was no assignment.

One of the unpleasant aspects of hanging around Camp Upton was that unassigned barracks were assigned KP (Kitchen Police) duty on a regular basis. This meant reporting to the Mess Hall at 5:30 A.M. and working there until 8:00 P.M. My barracks was being called about every other day and I dreaded the wakeup call at 4:30 in the morning which meant KP duty for that day.

Fortunately, there is always somebody in any organization who knows how to beat the system. The fellow on the bunk next to mine noticed how victims were routed out of the barracks in the dark and roll call wasn't taken until after they had arrived at the Mess Hall. Since assignments were random, there was no fixed count to the number of men reporting for duty. He pointed out to me that we could straggle to the end of the column and disappear into the furnace room of the building as the group rounded a corner going to the kitchen. All we had to do was wait until the barracks had been checked by the inspecting officer and then spend the rest of the day at the PX (Post Exchange) or go back to the barracks later in the day. All unassigned personnel had that privilege.

The ploy worked like a charm. The only hazard would be a slob on the serving line who might recognize us as being from his barracks. That wasn't likely since people moved in and out regularly. After three weeks, I was finally ordered to board a train leaving the camp. As the train started south, I was confident it would end up in New Jersey and I would be stationed near home. But train kept going south, past Pennsylvania, and I started to worry. The train was very slow and we arrived at the destination at night. The sign said "Fort Bragg" and the location was Fayetteville, North Carolina. The sign underneath really rattled me, reading "Field Artillery Replacement Training Center."

Field Artillery!? What in the world was the sense in sending me here? After we were assigned to a company and settled in our barracks, the entire plan was explained to us the following morning. At Camp Upton, selection had been made of all personnel with minor and major physical disabilities. A company of 240 men had been put together and were to be subjected to rigorous infantry basic training to determine if they could be assigned to combat duty if necessary. It seemed that war casualties had been higher than expected and some emergency reserves might be needed. We were an experimental group and would be given physical exams every week to determine if we would hold up under such tough training. But what was I doing there? I had "Limited Service" stamped on my papers. In typical Army fashion, I was told to take the matter up with my commanding officer. I might as well have protested to a brick wall. So, moaning and groaning, I began the infantry basic training regimen.

Infantry basic training was very harsh but it did strengthen my body. Several men were taken out of the group after they showed symptoms of respiratory or cardiac distress. One poor fellow actually had a real heart attack after a long hike with a fully loaded knapsack.

As part of the training, we had to qualify with the rifle on the target range. We were given World War I Enfield 30 caliber rifles. These happened to be very accurate weapons with a calibrated aiming site. When we got to the range, I had to take off my glasses to aim the weapon. The gunnery sergeant said to aim at the bullseye 200 yards away. I informed the sergeant I could not make out the bullseye or any other part of the target. He asked me what I did see and I replied all I could make out was a dull gray blur. He wasn't at all fazed and ordered me to shoot my ten rounds at the blur. All the others were trying to focus on the bullseye and were jittery in aiming their weapons. Since I couldn't see anything, I was relaxed and perfectly steady and fired off ten shots without really caring where they went. After completing the course, the flag went up at the target indicating several bullseyes. The sergeant stared at me in disbelief and entered the notation "Marksman" on my official Army record. That classification proved to be a disaster in my later military life.

Shortly before the end of the training session, the Army announced a program had been started to send selected personnel to various colleges and universities to study certain subjects having military applications. The program was called the Army Specialized Training Program (ASTP). Selection would be by competitive examination. I applied immediately and took the qualification exam. It was a three hour grilling covering everything from vocabulary to map reading. Unfortunately, I had never been a Boy Scout and had never been exposed to terrain and contour maps. However, I managed to obtain the required score and was accepted into the program. A group of us were sent to the Citadel in Charleston, South Carolina, for additional testing and assignment to a particular course. After two weeks at the Citadel I was assigned to the University of Kentucky at Lexington, Kentucky, to take the special advanced electrical engineering program. There would be five three-month semesters, with no breaks, to complete the program.

The course began in April of 1943. Life at University of Kentucky was quite pleasant. The courses were intensive but I found them compatible with my capabilities and I maintained a good grade level. We had very little time for any social interaction with the female students but we were just about the only men on the campus. They had set up Saturday dances as recreation for the troops which were poorly attended. Upon questioning, many of the soldiers reported they were terrible dancers or had never learned to dance, which was my status. The army response was typical - there would be compulsory ballroom dancing instruction added to the regular classroom schedule on Saturday mornings and all troops would participate. A number of the girls volunteered to risk having their toes crushed under heavy army boots as partners for the dancing lessons. It was a peculiar experience. We had to wear standard array issue combat boots and still learn to step lightly while learning to dance the fox trot, lindy hop, waltz, and something called the peabody. Anyway, we got to meet some of the girls at these dances; they were very nice but quite reserved.

Army personnel were assigned two to a dormitory room. Each soldier had his own bed and study desk. Classes began at 8:00 A.M. and lasted until 5:00 P.M. on weekdays and 8:00 A.M. to Noon on Saturdays. We had the rest of Saturday and all Sunday free. There were a surprising number of Jewish families in Lexington. Most of them were very prosperous, having horse stables and large estates. Every so often, an invitation would be extended to the Jewish soldiers to have dinner with one of the families on some special occasion. The chauffeured limousine would come up to the dormitory to pick up the guests. I went to two of these dinners and was quite impressed with their luxurious surroundings.

One of the difficulties was the matter of courtesy. We were told it would be improper to refuse any of the food offered to us. The food was great but they would have as many as five entrees on the table and the servants would pile the stuff on our plates with a vengeance. After bloating our stomachs we were taken in the limo for a tour of the stables and the estate. Then we would be taken back to the ballroom to dance with some young ladies who also had been invited to dinner. Coming from a poor family in Brooklyn, I felt somewhat jealous of these people who had never known hardship in their entire lives. Still, they were warm and friendly and put on no airs in their attitude toward the soldiers. I'm glad they didn't ask me to ride one of the horses - that would have been sheer disaster.

The advanced engineering groups were allowed to complete their programs while most of the soldiers left to join active military units. By the end of the summer of 1944, there were only 15 of us in the electrical engineering program who actually got certificates of completion. We completed our studies at the end of August 1944, and were required to undergo a graduation physical exam by the civilian school doctor. After examining me he noticed the notation "Limited Service" on my record. I informed him it was a restriction to service on mainland U.S.A. because of defective eyesight. He looked at me, saw the notation "Marksman" on my military record and threw a book at me. He asked me to start reading and when I did so, he proceeded to cross out the limited duty notation. He said if I had made Marksman, passed the engineering course and could read without difficulty, there should be no restrictions on my future military service. I protested to no avail and lost my cherished obstacle to overseas duty. Four months later, I was on my way to the South Pacific.

Anyway, we were promoted to the glorious rank of private first class upon graduation. Then the army announced the complete cancellation of the program and the assignment of the graduates to various branches of the army in alphabetical order. When it came to my turn, the orders read "Army Ordnance Depot, Flora, Mississippi." That was quite a blow. One interesting assignment was for two members of my class who had Master's degrees from previous education but had concealed this information to get into the

ASTP program. They revealed their previous education upon graduation and were assigned immediately to a strange place called Oak Ridge, Tennessee, with no army organization identification. It wasn't until years later I learned about the atomic bomb development group at that location. The prospect of going to a hellhole in Mississippi was a rude ending to my stay at a college dormitory.

When I arrived at Flora, Mississippi, I met 18 other graduates of the ASTP electrical engineering program who had been sent to this rathole. We were assembled into a room for assignment and were told there were urgent openings in two specialties - ammunition handlers and blacksmiths. Upon questioning, the officer described the job of ammunition handler as requiring little manual work and enjoying rapid promotion. It consisted mainly of removing damaged fuses from artillery shells that didn't explode upon landing on their target. The rapid promotion involved replacing people who had some problem in removing a fuse. Every so often, the shell would explode during the fuse removal procedure. That job certainly did not appeal to me.

The other job sounded even worse. The ordnance department operates giant cranes which can lift tanks and other heavy equipment. These cranes use a huge hook to lift the heavy steel cables which are placed around the load. After the hooks are manufactured or reconditioned, there are residual stresses left inside the steel. The ordnance blacksmiths place the hook into a gas blast furnace to get them white hot, then remove the hook to an anvil and beat the hook with sledge hammers for hours to relieve the stresses. The hook is reinserted into the furnace periodically to maintain the white hot temperature. I couldn't believe this sort of torture actually was a part of the army list of occupational specialties.

As luck would have it, they suddenly announced a few openings in tracked vehicle school for experienced mechanics. I raised my hand immediately despite the fact I never had owned or repaired a vehicle in my life. However, I knew the theory of internal combustion engines and knew the army does everything by the numbers in technical training. Each student in the class was given a worn tank engine to be reconditioned and restored to combat service. At the end of the course, the engines would be started and checked for proper operation. Any student who couldn't repair the engine would be transferred to an infantry unit without delay. My plan was to observe the student next to me and follow his motions exactly as the training sergeant announced each operation and counted off the turns of a wrench or a screwdriver.

I managed to disassemble the engine without mishap and replaced the worn parts as directed. Grinding the valves was a bit tricky but I bluffed my way through that section. After the final assembly, the engines were to be tested the following morning. I knew in my bones my engine would not run. In desperation, I got a heavy wire and shorted out the starting battery. The next class was waiting outside for the next session. The instructor was in a hurry to finish the testing and start the next class. As he went down the line; the engines roared into operation, one after the other. As he came to mine, I pressed the starter button and only a click sounded. The sergeant stared at me and commented that there was no spare battery available to test the engine. Using my most persuasive vocabulary, I convinced the sergeant my engine was perfectly restored and it wouldn't be necessary to go hunting for a battery to prove the point. Under pressure of time, he approved my work and I got a reprieve.

After that nerve-wracking experience, the nineteen graduates of the ASTP assembled in the PX to drown their frustrations in a beer marathon. One of the men, a very sharp individual named Goddard, announced he would send a telegram to the head of the Signal Corps, General Parker, Chief Signal Officer, telling him a group of electrical engineering graduates of the ASTP were wasting their time and the army's time in the Mississippi ordnance depot. When the local command heard of this unauthorized tactic, they threatened to court martial the whole lot of us. But, a few days later, the order came through to transfer all nineteen of us to the Special Signal Corps School at Philadelphia, Pennsylvania, without delay.

Back to civilization at last! We were given authorization to travel by rail to our destination. The train station at Jackson, Mississippi was in turmoil. There were no seats available on any train going north. Corporal Goddard was amazing. He got hold of the station manager and wove a tale of a secret mission vital to ending the war and was of the utmost urgency. Not only did we get on the train, but we bounced several people from their compartments and traveled in style to Philadelphia.

When we arrived at Philadelphia, we were taken to the Upper Darby Country Club. Our delight at this opportunity was tempered when we learned our only contact with the country club was to use the club gymnasium for our sleeping quarters. Rows of army cots had been laid out on the floor of the basketball court. Our entire day would be spent at Hog Island in South Philadelphia. We would undergo an intensive training program for three weeks on special equipment and then be sent on to an unknown destination.

The facilities at Hog Island were not what I associated with standard Signal Corps equipment. Everything was big - large high powered commercial radio transmitters, massive 100 foot high towers, huge diesel-driven generators, and my first view of radar equipment. There were two radar installations, one with the earliest technology of a single baseline on the face of a cathode ray tube, and a later version using a massive rotating antenna assembly on the roof of a circular sweep of the trace on a cathode ray tube. The antenna, casually called a "bedspring," was a very large rectangular array of short rods called dipoles, all supported by a single shaft interconnected by a heavy motor mounted inside the roof of the trailer. The momentum of the rotating antenna caused the trailer to rock back and forth and the operator would tend to get seasick from the motion.

This experience was fascinating but somewhat puzzling. At the end of training session, we were informed of our special assignment. The project was under the supervision of a special branch of the Signal Corps called the Communications Service, reporting directly to the Chief Signal Officer in Washington. We were to construct major communication installations at locations revealed when we arrived there.

In November of 1944, we boarded a train west. The train was very slow and took more than a week to reach the West coast. The prevailing rumor was that we would end up in Honolulu, flown to Hawaii on transport planes. When we arrived at San Francisco, we were taken by ferry to Angel Island, which was then a major port of embarkation for troop ships. So much for any chance of flying.

The troopship was the U.S.S. General Hersey, containing 6,000 soldiers. Sleeping facilities were arrays of five canvas bunks on top of each other on every deck. There would be two meals a day; most of the time would be spent waiting in line for the meal. My bunk was the top level on a location in F deck, two levels below the waterline. The heat from all those bodies crammed together was stifling. An oscillating fan on a nearby post gave me a breath of air about every thirty seconds.

On the first morning out, alarms started ringing about 5:30 A.M. and the loudspeaker called for somebody named "General Quarters." I didn't know what was going on and rolled out of the bunk and tried to open the bulkhead door. The door didn't open and I assumed it just needed some lubrication. Later that day, one of the sailors told me the ship had lifeboats for only 4,000 men, and S and F decks were locked up in any emergency. The men in those locations were to be expendable. With this news, I spent the rest of the journey sleeping on the anchor chain on top deck. I went below only to stand in line for meals. The ship zigzagged all over the Pacific Ocean. After several days, I asked one of the sailors how long it would take us to get to Hawaii. If not Hawaii, I was sure the destination should be one of the exotic tropical islands. He laughed and pointed to the rolling wake in the ocean behind the ship.

I should have known better. The trip took 27 days and we anchored off the coast of Dutch New Guinea at Hollandia. We climbed down rope ladders to a bobbing landing craft and were dumped onto a lonely beach. The hours passed by and nobody came to pick us up. By late afternoon, the hunger pangs were serious and a small group set out to find some unit to give us some food. They located a Seabee unit further down the beach and came back with small cans of Australian mutton. When I tried to open my can, the lid stuck to the contents like glue. Canned mutton is mainly fat with a vein of tough stringy meat embedded in the fat. We were so hungry we ate the horrible slop. By nightfall, a truck came by to take us to the replacement depot. This was a huge tent camp with continuous soldiers arriving and departing as they were assigned. While waiting for assignment, I got the job of night telephone operator at the camp switchboard. That was the closest I ever came to telephone work in my Army career.

We waited and waited and no assignment came through. Meanwhile, my tent bunkmate, a hustler from Chicago named Siegel, came up with an interesting scam. The tents had no lighting whatsoever. When troops arrived late at night, the desk sergeant would obtain some candles from the supply depot to light their way while they settled down in their tents. Our scam was to call the supply room at night, tap on the switchboard to simulate a typewriter, pretend to be the receiving office, and request a supply of candles for a large contingent arriving at the camp. The ruse worked great. We got two cases of candles and proceeded to sell them to incoming troops at a guilder a candle. We were required by international agreement to use the local currency and had to change our dollars into guilders at two guilders per dollar. The scam netted us about a hundred dollars, which was very big money to a private first class. But once you start with a criminal attitude, it becomes worse as you see the money roll in.

We ran out of candles in a short time, but my nefarious buddy Siegel dreamed up another scam to swindle the troops. There were many empty beer cans in the trash bins around the camp. There was also a gasoline supply dump with valves fitted into 55-gallon drums to fuel the many trucks constantly running in and out of the camp. Siegel came up with an empty five-gallon gas can and filled it with gasoline. He scrounged a wad of fiberglass from a wrecked plane and proceeded to make wicks out of them. We filled the beer cans with high octane gasoline, stuck fiberglass wicks into the cans and sold them as approved replacements for the unavailable candles. The swindle worked for two nights until one can tipped over and set fire to one of the tents.

The subsequent investigation nailed us as the culprits and we were assigned a week's KP duty as punishment. Siegel started to talk about stealing things like canned fruit to sell to the troops but I refused to do anything more that smelled like a scam. I was finished with my criminal career. Somehow, I think Siegel maneuvered himself into some black market operation later in his military career. He was always dreaming of the big one - a master swindle could make him a rich man. We were assigned to different units and I never saw him again.

At last a permanent assignment came through and a group of 300 men was assembled at the replacement center. We were told we were now the 3367th Signal Service Battalion and would be shipped to the island of Luzon in the Philippine Islands for our first major assignment. The trip to Luzon took forever. We boarded a flat bottom LCI (Landing Craft Infantry) at Hollandia and rocked and rolled our way first to the island of Leyte through the North China Sea. Everybody got sick on that trip. We had to wait on Leyte until another landing craft would be available for the trip to Luzon.

While on Leyte, we had one of those incidents existing only in comic books. A soldier came into our camp and reported Japanese soldiers had been seen coming down from the mountaintop. Our officers became frantic and set up two perimeter lines to meet the dangerous enemy. Then they sent a jeep with two of our men to find some fighting type soldiers who could defend the inexperienced Signal Corps troops. They found an infantry unit further on down the hill and were very embarrassed to request their protection. After enduring a huge horse laugh from the combat troops, we told them where the enemy soldiers were located. We learned the Japanese soldiers had been holed up in a bunker for weeks and were sick and starving. They were looking to surrender to any unit that could feed them. Imagine, I could have been a war hero capturing a band of Japanese soldiers single-handedly. During that emergency, I learned the weapon I had been carrying since leaving the U.S. was defective. I tried to test the carbine with a live cartridge and it wouldn't fire because of a defective firing pin. So much for my frontline effectiveness.

We finally made the trip to Luzon and set up camp near the Far East Air headquarters at Clark Field. Our assignment was to construct and set into operation the main weather station for the Air Force in the Philippine Islands. However, when our officers were called into the first planning session with the top Air Force brass, they came out with a surprising story. This was to be a top level facility and high level brass would be living here. Since it was essentially a hot jungle environment, the top priority was a full size swimming pool for the general staff officers.

We had been trained in heavy construction but nobody knew anything about swimming pools. The Air Force supplied us with specifications for the large pool and we would have no difficulty in that aspect of the project. The main problem was how to fill the pool since the nearest lake was twelve miles away. Their solution was simple - run a twelve-mile pipeline from the lake to the camp. A transport plane was dispatched from California under the highest priority containing twelve miles of pipe and manuals on the necessary plumbing to make a permanent water supply. There we were, an entire Signal Corps battalion, laying pipe in the jungle and bolting the 20-foot sections together. At the lake, we set up a pumping and purification unit. At the camp, we had to provide a water supply for the pool as well as for the top brass living quarters. The war was becoming a very peculiar affair.

After the pool was built, we started work full blast on the weather station. It was a large installation with radio equipment, teletypewriters and encoding equipment. I worked on the Moorehead

Keyer, an interesting coding and decoding machine used to scramble radio teletype messages. The job went smoothly and we turned over the installation to the Air Force for operation.

In cleaning up the area, I managed to forget my tool kit which had been left under the coding machine. After the turnover, I went to the coding room to get my tools back. The guard at the door reminded me it was now a secret installation and I had no clearance to enter the room. I argued I had built and tested the damn machine and I needed my tool kit. He pointed his rifle at me and told me where I could go.

Months later, a high level officer from Army Intelligence came to the camp and asked to see me. He produced a batch of rusty tools and a torn up leather case with my name on it. He said these were unauthorized items found in a top level classified location and they pointed to me as the culprit. The tools had been x-rayed and dunked into an acid bath to determine if there was any secret writing on them. I told the major they were indeed my tools and I had risked death trying to get them back. They were now totally useless and I suggested throwing them into the trash barrel. I had obtained a replacement kit after my encounter with the guard. The intelligence officer seemed very disappointed. Fortunately, I had been given security clearance before working at that station and the matter was dropped. I still felt the war was taking strange turns.

After finishing the weather station, we were called together and were told the real reason behind our strange organization. The invasion of Japan was being planned and massive bombing raids were to be made prior to the invasion. The problem was the Japanese anti-aircraft fire was becoming very accurate and we were losing too many planes and pilots in the bombing raids. The planes could be replaced but the loss in pilots was critical.

The secret project was to use pilot-less bombers to fly (
target areas under precise radio control and release their bon
also under radio control. The planes were already being
manufactured but the radio system had to be built from scratch.
There were to be three powerful radio stations, one in the
Philippines, one in Kunming, China, and one in India. The radio
beacons had to be extremely narrow and very powerful. The radio
control beacon was to be built in the Philippines and that was our
job. The project involved constructing a powerful transmitter station
and a massive array of 52 diamond-shaped rhombic antennas in a
straight line extending over a mile.

Each antenna section was to be supported by four 100-foot tall
towers, each anchored to the ground with three steel cables
connected to anchor rods buried eight feet into the ground. The
towers and the antennas were to be made in an assembly line using
Filipino labor. Our job was to erect the towers, connect the antennas,
build the transmitter station and set the system into operation. The
output beam was to be pencil-thin and powerful enough to fry any
birds coming into its path. The entire battalion of 300 men was to
work sixteen hours a day and seven days a week to meet the target
turnover date of December 7, 1945, a very significant time frame.

For each tower, the ground had to be cleared and leveled, and a
concrete base poured. To secure the wire cables, a hole had to be
blown into the ground to make an opening about a foot wide and
eight feet deep to hold the anchor rods. Each tower required three
rods spaced equally around the tower. The digging crews had to
chop pilot holes into the rock hard ground in order to place the
explosives. Of course, I was assigned to one of the digging crews
and it was terrible work in the hot humid tropical environment.
However, we had some experienced construction men in the crew

and one of them showed me how to unwrap dynamite sticks and shape the nitroglycerin-soaked clay into a cone-shaped explosive that could blow a hole with a controlled diameter at a predetermined angle.

I applied immediately for the job of blastman. After the digging crew had toiled miserably to poke the pilot holes, I would place my carefully shaped charges into the hole, insert the blasting cap, unroll my hundred feet of wire and connect the wires to my plunger-operated magneto which would generate the electric spark.

The traditional procedure of the blastman is to cry "Fire in the hole!" three times and point in the downwind direction to warn anybody in the path of flying debris. Then I would depress the plunger and see a small cloud of dust come out of the hole, which was now about a foot wide, eight feet deep and at an angle of 60 degrees. The job required very little effort and I could sit in the shade while the others sweated in the hot sun.

My job as a blastman was too good to last. I found I couldn't sleep well and was very jittery. I went on sick call and the doctor noticed my pupils were dilated. He was ready to have me jailed for drug use when I explained I was a blastman on the digging crew. He wanted to know what kind of rubber gloves I used while shaping the clay. Seeing my blank face, he was astonished I had not been warned of the effect of absorbing nitroglycerin into the skin. I was suffering from nitroglycerin poisoning and was bucking for a heart attack. I was ordered to leave that job and not touch explosives any more.

Not wishing to go back to the digging crew, I obtained the job of sanitary engineer for the camp. The job entailed disposing of the residues from the camp mess hall and maintaining the separate latrine facilities for the officers and for the enlisted personnel. I was one of the few people left in camp while most of the men went out to the antenna field. My primary responsibility was the proper disposal of the kitchen waste, particularly the smelly debris from butchering the meat. I would transport the waste from the mess hall to a large garbage pit and cover it with my secret mixture of used motor oil and high octane gasoline. When ignited, the pile would burn with a low flame and would be reduced to a fine ash. I was quite proud of my skill in keeping the residue level very low in the pit. I used this mixture also to burn away the residues from our 16-hole latrine. I had the same success in keeping the low level in the latrine.

However, nothing ever goes right in the army for long. I had a daily requirement of two gallons of used motor oil which I obtained from the motor pool. All went well until they ran out of used motor oil. I requested fresh oil but was refused any oil by the motor pool sergeant. I was left only with high gasoline and very hot weather. The situation wasn't going according to my routine but I had to dispose of the daily waste.

The latrine had solid hardwood boards with smoothly sanded seat openings. The outer frame was firmly constructed with corner posts and burlap sides. Shade was provided by a corrugated tin roof. With some trepidation, I poured my five gallons of gasoline over the waste and stretched a long gasoline-soaked cord to a spot about 30 feet as a precaution. I didn't know what to expect. I lit the cord and waited for the results. There was a loud explosion and a sheet of flame leaped into the air. The entire facility disappeared in a matter of minutes.

I went to the orderly room where the company commander sat behind his desk. I walked in, saluted smartly and requested a four-man digging crew to construct a latrine. He said we already had a satisfactory facility and inquired what was with the existing one. With a straight face, I replied it was no longer usable, being on fire. I placed all the blame on the motor pool sergeant but the captain didn't buy my story. The replacement unit was never as comfortable as the old one. We couldn't get the right kind of wood for that smooth finish.

Just about that time, the company clerk developed a case of typhus and was sent back to the States. I immediately claimed to be a skilled typist and took over the job of company clerk. It appeared to be a soft touch until I realized there was more to the job than typing reports. About two miles south of camp was the village of Alabang, where the main source of income was a brothel which served army personnel. There was no medical supervision of the women or the clientele and venereal disease was rampant. When I saw the confidential file on how many of our troops had to go into Manila for treatment of their disease, it took major juggling to maintain the necessary manpower for the construction crews.

After a while, the job settled down to a routine and I got along well with the captain. My desk was in a corner of his office and I became a reasonably fast hunt-and-peck typist. One advantage of the job was assigning men to twelve man teams to set up primary communications in certain combat areas. This became a second responsibility of the company after a large number of men were released from the antenna project. It was very simple to add my name to the list after each team went out. Those assignments added points to my service record for any future priority in getting out of the army.

Work on the transmitter station continued into the late summer of 1945. The war in Europe had ended in May and we were wondering when the war with Japan would ever end. The prospect of a land invasion of Japan was frightening. The station was just about ready for test in August of 1945. However, strange events took over. About the third week in August, we received notice to stop work on the station. The rumors circulated thick and fast that something big had happened but we had no firm information about any new military operation or weapon. It took a few days to learn the atomic bomb had been dropped on Hiroshima and Nagasaki and Japan had surrendered.

The relief on everyone's face was almost tangible – no costly invasion, no more injuries and deaths and, best of all, return home to the mainland. If anybody ever questions the propriety of dropping bombs, they should talk to the soldiers and sailors who lived only because that weapon terminated the war. We considered it one of the greatest moments in history.

The station had been completed and tested and we awaited further order for its operation. I should have known the military mind thinks in strange ways. An order came down from top level that the entire project was to be blown up and buried to the point there should be no trace of any activity that may have occurred in the area. Since it was a top-secret project and never declassified, all records, drawings, equipment, towers, and antennas had to be totally destroyed. The army rules on security were rigid; it was the approach to terminating highly classified operations.

We spent the next weeks dynamiting everything. We borrowed a bulldozer from the Navy Seabees outfit and dutifully dug a huge hole and buried all the hardware. When we were finished, all that could be seen was the original rice paddy without a trace of any rice plants. I felt very disappointed in having nothing to show for the months of concentrated effort that went into the project. Anyway, the feeling passed and the next objective was how to leave the island and get home to the U.S. Since we were a service organization and not a combat unit, we had a low priority on transportation back to the U.S.

While we waited through September and October, the captain offered me a deal.

If I volunteered to stay on, he would take me with him to Japan, where he had orders to go through the islands and modify the Japanese radio equipment for U.S. military use. I would get a staff sergeant rating and would have a blank check in drawing rations from U.S. Army Air Force bases. The assignment would entail traveling the entire length of Japan.

If I had no obligations at home, it would have been a dream assignment. But my mother's letters complained she was having a difficult time surviving on the allocations from my pay and Harold's death benefit. She wanted me to resume my job to have a decent income. Furthermore, I was convinced the Japanese people would seek revenge on all U.S. troops. With everything going on, I politely refused the offer and said I had enough of Army life. I wanted to go home.

The problem was getting on a ship to go to the processing center in Guam. The first choice of travel was given to combat personnel and injured or sick troops. At the rate of ship departures, we wouldn't get home until 1946. I came up with the dirty plan to get us out of the Philippines. We had a subsidiary outfit on the island of Guam. I sent them a teletype message inquiring about the terrible typhoon had struck the island. The response came back, "What typhoon?" I replied "The typhoon that knocked down your communication tower WHICH HAD TO BE REBUILT AS AN URGENT MILITARY REQUIREMENT." It was sheer coincidence we had a team of twelve specialists in tower construction at our camp. My name happened to be on the list. The underlying message was that an emergency crew had to be sent from the Philippines to Guam to repair the supposed damage.

The scheme worked. An authorization came through ordering twelve tower construction specialists to proceed to Guam with top priority to repair the towers. We had to displace twelve veteran infantrymen to get on the next troopship. It was dirty pool but drastic means were needed for a drastic situation. Twelve of us boarded a modified tanker ship in November of 1945 and no matter where we went on the ship, it smelled from its last oil cargo. We landed in Guam early in December, 1945. We had to wait a week or so for transportation to the island of Saipan, where the discharge processing center was located.

While on Guam, I wandered over to the dock and noticed a huge pile of large crates being loaded onto a barge and dumped into the bay to form a breakwater. The crates contained new unused radio transmitter equipment. I was told the contracts with the government by the manufacturers specified any equipment delivered to the military must never reappear on the domestic or foreign market, even if never used. As surplus items, they would depress the prices of new equipment. So, Guam had the most expensive protected port in the world.

At the end of December we obtained transportation to Saipan and we were processed for return to the mainland. A small group of us were assigned to a Navy attack transport vessel for the trip home. The captain of the ship told us we were guests of the navy and would have no duty assignments while on board. Between the hearty fresh food and all the free time, it was like a luxury cruise. The delightful voyage took about a week to reach Los Angeles. After arriving in California, a group of about 50 soldiers whose homes were on the east coast were packed into an old army transport plane. The pilot was a grey-haired retired veteran pilot from a commercial line. We sat on long benches in the cargo compartment with one blanket each to keep warm. There was no heat in the cargo area.

The plane took off without incident and I was looking forward to my discharge after three years of military service. Somewhere above Tennessee, the pilot announced the wings were icing up and there was a hydraulic leak in one of the engines. We would have to land for the necessary repairs. It was the middle of the winter and miserably cold. We set down on an abandoned airstrip of a former Air Force base. All the troops had to get out and help push the huge plane into a hangar. We waited all night for a repair crew to turn up.

Early the next morning, a crew arrived with a couple of electric dryers and dozens of wiping cloths. While the Air Force personnel repaired the leak, all the passengers had to wipe down the wings to remove any trace of ice or moisture. Finally, all of us had to push the plane back onto the runway and get back in for the last leg of the flight. We arrived at Maguire Air Force Base in New Jersey on January 4 and I was officially discharged on January 6, 1946. During the final processing, I learned an error had been made in the code identifying my occupational specialty when I first came in to Camp Upton. Instead of the code for Telephone Central Office Installer, I had been given the handle of "Fixed Station Radio Repairman." That was one of the reasons I never saw Fort Monmouth or Camp Crowder. Oh well, water under the bridge.

Karen's comment:

Learning about Sid's war experiences through his writing was fascinating for me; his grasp of detail amazing. It's hard to understand what these young men (and women) went through - yet so universal. Like many WWII veterans, Sid rarely discussed his actions after his military career ended. He served his country.

My father's eldest brother, Harold William Vogel, died at age 24 while in military service. He was killed at sea as part of the "friendly-fire" destruction of the U.S.S. Langley ordered by the War Department. It was a communications disaster covered up by the U.S. government until a lawsuit filed by the soldiers' families unveiled the true episode after the war ended. Harold was initially declared missing in action on February 27, 1942. His date of death was later assigned by the Army as December 18, 1945 in order to provide death benefits income to his mother. Sid never recovered from the death of his idolized brother. He rarely mentioned Harold but made sure I knew what happened decades ago.

It is difficult to find official documentation of the incident. *Pawns of War: The Loss of the USS Langley and the USS Pecos*[4], written in 1983, details the disaster and lists Harold Vogel's name among the men who lost their lives due to incompetent leadership. I purchased the book for my father. He read it immediately from cover to cover, gratified that the story was finally validated. When my father was dying (at age 95) I told him he would be able to see Harold again; I think it gave him comfort.

---

[4] *www.amazon.com/Pawns-War-Loss-Langley-Pecos/dp/0870215159/ref=sr_1_1?keywords=uss+langley&qid=15565152 57&s=gateway&sr=8-1*

Chapter 8

Post-War Life

Sid:

Soon after I got home from military service, I sent a letter to the local Western Electric office to let them know I was ready to go back to work. Although veterans were eligible to collect $20 a month for 52 weeks while looking for a job, I refused to take anything while I waited for my first postwar assignment. The reply came less than a week later, to report to the central office in Queens, New York. The letter informed me I was eligible for all the wage increases made during the war. I would be reinstated at the magnificent rate of $1.08 an hour.

Upon arriving at the job site, I learned a school had been set up to train testers and trouble-shooters for growth. It was going to balloon after years of stagnation. I was assigned to the first class of the school, which provided three weeks of intensive training in the type of electromechanical system which was most common all over the country. It was called the "panel" switching system. The instruction was very thorough and I was confident I could hold my own in debugging any problems.

After completing the schooling, I was given my first job assignment as a system tester and trouble-shooter to report to the central office on Troy Avenue in Brooklyn. When I walked into the office, I was stunned. The equipment was totally different and I had never even heard of the system. It seems the new type of switching system had been developed by the Bell Telephone Laboratories prior to the war and a prototype had been built at this location just before the war. With the end of the war, the new system was to be updated and placed into service. I was to be the trouble-shooter on the job.

Fortunately, the Laboratories had prepared comprehensive documentation and I grabbed every bit of support data I could find. I took the documents and system drawings home every night and pored over them for hours until I could comprehend the control logic behind the system. It took me about a week before I started to make myself useful. I told the job supervisor about my predicament. His reply was "a good tester should be able to diagnose any system by sheer instinct." He was no help.

Later on, I was apprenticed to a brilliant circuit analyst named Curtis Fisher. He was a fantastic teacher and I really learned how to locate and clear troubles in almost any designed system. I accompanied Curtis from job to job and prepared a little black book containing all the tricks and shortcuts all testers use to expedite turnover of the central office. When we would solve a particularly difficult problem, he would take the time to review with me every step we had taken to analyze the situation and how we could do the next job more efficiently. In later years, I learned my brilliant tutor had developed a brain tumor and had been severely compromised. What a terrible end for such a bright person! After a while, I could handle job problems on my own and qualified as an overall system analyst.

Karen's comment:

I was an advocate, in both a personal and professional role, for my friend Laura who developed a glioblastoma, an aggressive type of brain cancer. Sid frequently asked about Laura and expressed concern about her situation. He understood my involvement to enhance the quality of her life. She cooked "real" potato latkes for

Sid when she accompanied me on a December 2016 visit, he happily devoured them. Laura died 4 months after Sid, 30 months after her diagnosis. I like the image of them in a well-stocked kitchen somewhere, enjoying a good meal together.

Chapter 9

Romantic Awakening

Sid:
Western Electric had bridged my military service with my civilian service to give me sufficient time for a two-week vacation in 1946. At age 24, this was to be my first real vacation and I decided to avoid the height of the hay fever season in New York by north to New Hampshire which was supposedly free of ragweed. I had suffered "summer colds" from childhood and was diagnosed in my late teens as sensitive to ragweed. After reading the ads in a newspaper on vacation spots, I located a hotel in Bethlehem, New Hampshire which advertised cheap rates.

In late August, I took the train up to New England and rented a room at the Ferry House in Bethlehem, New Hampshire. It was old and a trifle smelly but the food was good and I didn't sneeze very much. The other residents were a contrasting collection of old Jews who conducted prayer services every afternoon and a small group of young people. There was one group of three girls staying at the hotel who drew my close attention. I didn't really know how to approach them and I was particularly interested in the shortest one who had beautiful black curly hair and a fabulous figure outlined by a tight polo shirt and shorts. I summoned up my courage to strike up a conversation with the girls and I learned they also lived in Brooklyn and had come up to Bethlehem also to escape the ragweed season.

I was delighted to find it easy to talk to the one I had singled out and the more time we spent together, the more I realized I was deeply attracted to her. She was bright, warm-hearted, had a wonderful sense of humor, and seemed to like my company. She even agreed to accompany me on a hike up Mount Agassiz despite wearing open-toed shoes. By the time we reached the top, she had ten bleeding toes. I learned there were two other men who were trying to lure her into marriage and I was faced with a crisis decision. If I didn't do something very soon, I might lose this wonderful person and might never find anybody like her. In the middle of the second week, I asked her if she would marry me. I promised her she would never regret her decision if she said yes. Somewhat to my surprise and to my utter delight, she agreed to marry me. Of course, that beautiful girl was Doris Reger, my loving wife.

Doris had come up to Bethlehem with her sister Edie, her cousin Lottie, and a close friend, Bella. One of her suitors, Carl, had followed her up to Bethlehem, but was staying at a different hotel. He came from a wealthy family in the tie business and was a dangerous rival for Doris' hand. We found a girl named Sydelle, who was staying with her mother also at the Perry House, who was on the prowl for a rich husband. We managed to introduce Sydelle to my rich rival and they seemed to click. Edie had come up to Bethlehem a few days after Doris and her group had arrived. Edie met Oscar Spilke, a businessman in the brassiere manufacturing line. He was staying at the Maplewood Hotel, a posh and more expensive location a few miles out of town. Anyway, by the time we were ready to go home, there were three engaged couples, Doris and Sidney, Edie and Oscar, and Sydelle and Carl.

When the returning train arrived at Grand Central Station, Doris' parents were waiting for us in their 1937 Dodge sedan. I was greeted with utter silence as Doris introduced me as the man she intended to marry. Very little was said on the trip back to Brooklyn but we held hands tightly and ignored the cold hostility in the air. It was worse when I got home and told my mother I was going to leave the house to get married. She was of the opinion I was too young to know what I was doing (at age 24) and that age 35 was more appropriate for marriage. I knew her concern was that I was her main support - my leaving would leave her only my dead brother's pension and a small Social Security check from my father's death. I promised to continue to help her if things became too critical. She did obtain a part-time job as a ticket taker in a small movie theatre to fill in the gap in her income. She soon met Doris and was well pleased with my choice.

Doris' family was concerned she would be marrying below her level. She was a licensed schoolteacher with a college degree and I was only an hourly rated technician. To quiet rumors of any possible misbehavior, we set our wedding date for the end of March 1947. As time went on, Doris' family warmed up to me and we got along well. Her father, Izzie Reger, was a housepainter who had once owned his own business but now worked for a contractor. Her mother, Fannie, was a traditional quiet housewife. They were both European born and still were not comfortable with modern dating patterns. The entire family, including an aunt and uncle and two cousins, lived in an old brownstone three story house on Vernon Avenue, which was only four blocks from where I lived on Greene Avenue. Doris even knew some of the boys who had gone to Boys High School with me.

Our engagement interval proved to me I had made a fabulous choice in the woman I was going to marry. She was all a man could ask for as a partner for life. The brownstone house had an outside stairway leading to a enclosed area between the outside and inside doors on the second floor. We used to sit there after an evening together and embrace. Under the moral code of that time, we could only hold each other closely and dream of the day when we could fulfill our passions completely as a married couple. I took many a cold shower during those months.

Tradition required the elder daughter (Edie) should be married first and then the younger daughter (Doris) could get married. To avoid any awkwardness the wedding was therefore planned as a double ceremony. The date was March 29, 1947. It was a very long wedding. The rabbi arrived late and the two ceremonies took forever. The guests from three families had exhausted the liquor supply before the ceremonies and I had to come up with enough money to get some more booze. Custom of the time was the bride's family paying for the room and dinner, and the groom's family paying for the liquor and flowers. Luckily, one of the guests owned a liquor store and we prevailed upon him to open the store and bring in another case of whiskey. The wedding took so long we lost our reservation at a nice hotel and had to settle for a tiny room at the Bossert Hotel in downtown Brooklyn. The room really didn't matter as long as we were together at last.

Karen's comment:

Summer resorts in the Catskill Mountains and New England were located in the "Borscht Belt," also known as the "Jewish Alps." (Borscht is a beet soup associated with eastern European immigrants.) The resorts were affordable, safe and popular spots for vacations (and courting) from the 1940s through 1960s. Food was prepared according to Jewish cultural preferences. Resorts hosted comedians and musicians who tested material and later became famous, including Joan Rivers, Mel Brooks and Billy Crystal.

My parents were married for 66 years, fondly described by Sid as "61 very happy years and 5 years not so great." Since the wedding ceremony wasn't finished until after midnight, they couldn't agree whether their anniversary was actually March 29 or 30. My parents were partners who balanced each other's strengths and although they sometimes had contradictory opinions, a true love story. My mother had strong views about personal accountability and didn't tolerate bad customer service. My father was the more social one; he enjoyed talking with all kinds of people but didn't like conflict. They were both witty skeptics, juggling funny comebacks. It took me a while to realize that yelling at each other was a form of affection. Watch any Woody Allen movie about marriage, that's my folks.

Chapter 10

Work and Family

Sid:

I had become active in the telephone workers union since I had returned from military service. Labor negotiations between the union and the Bell System management were not going well and there was the threat of a strike. As talks broke down, the strike seemed inevitable and a strike deadline was called for the first week in April 1947. I would be on my honeymoon during that week and I figured the strike would be over by the time we came back from our week in the Catskill Mountains. The strike lasted seven weeks and I had to be present on the picket line every day as the union shop steward.

One rainy evening, the downpour was fierce and the management wire chief for the building offered to take in the pickets and prepare coffee for them while sitting out the storm. We were going to accept the offer when the police sergeant monitoring the line blocked the doorway and announced nobody on the picket line could enter the building. He was dressed in a waterproof slicker and claimed as long as he had to stand in the rain, we had to stand in the rain, prepared or not. Without raingear I managed to catch a bad cold that night and spent the next few days as a bedridden invalid.

The supervisor at the strike job site was one of the very few Jewish men in the company. His name was Lou Lazarus. Each day of the strike, Lou would ask me which of the men were hurting the most during the strike. I picked out those who were married and had children. He would take one of the men to a hearty lunch each day and slip a few dollars in his pocket. I figured Lou must have spent close to a thousand dollars of his own money during the seven weeks of the strike. After the strike, the company would send time study engineers to Lou's jobs to find out why his operations always came in on time, always below budget and always without any manpower problems. They never understood how important it was to be a "mensch." After seven weeks, the union essentially lost the strike and settled for a nominal wage increase of four cents an hour. Lou was the one who later submitted my name for a vacancy on the installation engineering group at the company headquarters in New York.

Doris and I looked for an apartment we could afford but none were to be had. Postwar housing was totally inadequate to handle the surge of returning servicemen looking for a place to live. I moved into Doris' original bedroom on the third floor of her grandmother's brownstone. It was quite a tiny room, about six by ten feet. Her parents occupied the large bedroom on the third floor. Her aunt and uncle, Minnie and Abe Lucks, lived on the second floor with their children Artie and Lottie. Grandma Clara also slept on the second floor. The first floor had an enormous kitchen and a large room which was designed originally as the music room. There was a tiny enclosure containing a toilet facing the back yard. A bathtub and sink had been installed in a separate room off the kitchen. We shared a bathroom on the third floor.

During the strike, Doris went off to work each morning to teach elementary school, and I would hang around the house until my night shift picket duty. Her parents were convinced she had married a chronic loafer and were very distant to me during that time. However, they became more receptive after I returned to work. About a year after we moved in, her other uncle, Dave Lucks, had found a cheap private home in Flatbush for sale. He was a real estate salesman and was on the lookout for such a deal. The Lucks family moved to Flatbush and Izzie and Fanny moved down to the second floor. Thus, we had our own apartment on the third floor and we moved into the large bedroom.

In 1948, Doris developed a cyst on the base of her spine and had to have spinal surgery. She had a long recuperation period at home and was very bored. The first postwar television sets had come on the market with seven-inch and ten inch picture tubes. Dumont announced the development of a giant twelve inch tube and I decided to get the newest sets to give Doris some relief from her forced confinement. I had to reserve a demonstration of the twelve inch set which came only as a furniture console containing the black and white television set, a 78 rpm phonograph and a tube-type AM radio. I paid $727 for that console and was lucky to get delivery within the week. There were only two New York television stations in operation when we bought the set. Our giant twelve-inch screen was a novelty and we had many visitors to watch those early programs.

The old brownstone house had a tarred flat roof and no insulation between the roof and our apartment ceiling. The apartment was extremely hot in the summer, while the lower floors were cooler because of the thick brick walls between the old attached buildings. I read about the development of window air conditioner units for use in apartments. I bought one of the early units made by Carrier, a noisy bulky box which had to be fastened to the window sill. Fortunately, the old buildings had projecting stone windowsills and the air conditioner was mounted in the bedroom window resting on the sill. It drew an enormous amount of current but it did keep the bedroom cool. There were evenings when we would eat our dinner in the bedroom just to escape the heat.

We lived in that apartment for seven years. In 1949 Doris prevailed upon me to go back to school and finish my college education. I registered at the Polytechnic Institute of Brooklyn for the electrical engineering degree. It was a laborious grind with classes four nights a week from 6 PM to 10 PM. My weekends were spent in home assignments and drafting exercises. The problem with Brooklyn Poly was I had taken the courses several years before in the ASTP program and they wouldn't credit those courses because I had been away from school so long. My working hours alternated between day shifts and night shifts to match the type of installation. Modifications of central offices had to be done overnight. New offices and additions could only be done in the day shift. I would attend classes from 6 to 10 PM, then report for work at 11 PM. I had to cut down on some of the classes to prevent utter exhaustion.

In 1951, many things changed. Daniel was born in June and Doris went on maternity leave from her teaching job. In the fall, there was an opening in the headquarters engineering organization and my name was submitted for the position. I was summoned to report to the headquarters offices at 30 Church St., in lower Manhattan, and was grilled by several levels of management. After the intensive interviews, I felt my chances were not promising. I was going to college but didn't have a degree. It was a surprise when I found out later few of the staff engineers in the group had graduated college.

Anyway, about a week after the interviews, I was lying on the floor behind an equipment bay, tracking down a wiring error. I had just located the source of trouble when the job supervisor kicked the sole of my shoe and said there was someone who wanted to talk to me. I replied the trouble location was far more important than any conversation and he would just have to wait until I finished. The supervisor bent down and whispered,

"You stupid S.O.B., he's from headquarters. Get out from under there!"

I slid out and stared at the smiling countenance of Frank Stratford, Assistant Superintendent of Installation Engineering. He told me to show up at his office on Monday morning wearing a suit, white shirt, tie and black shoes. My application had been accepted.

Chapter 11

The Staff Engineer

Sid:

Working in the engineering office was a whole new way of life. As a field technician, I moved around a lot, climbed ladders, crawled under equipment bays, and used up a lot of energy. Now as a staff engineer, I had to sit in a chair all day with one break for lunch. For anybody coming in from the field, there was a standard introductory policy - one full year answering suggestions from the field. The company had a plan for rewarding any suggestions to improve efficiency or lower costs with a cash award amounting to ten percent of the first year's savings. This resulted in many harebrained ideas sent in with the hope of a cash bonanza. All suggestions had to be answered politely and technically accurate. In many cases, the installer would come up with a sensible idea which was already under development by the Bell Laboratories. My answer had to be congratulatory for the good idea and the refusal to pay had to be a gentle letdown.

Now with regular daytime hours, I could concentrate on steady attendance at the Brooklyn Poly night courses. The grind was fairly heavy, I tried to keep the program to three nights a week to give me some family life. Meanwhile, the Vernon Avenue neighborhood was deteriorating. In 1952, Doris and I decided to start looking for a home of our own in Long Island. We felt a home in the suburbs would be a better place to bring up our son. This required me to learn how to drive and buy a car for house hunting. My driving lessons were in a terribly congested section of Flushing and I had a tough time getting my license. I finally bought a 1947 Dodge sedan and parked it in the street next to Izzie's 1937 Dodge. Every weekend we went out in the car looking at houses. Daniel would be placed in a portable crib in the back seat.

We started out looking at areas in Long Island close to the Queens border. In 1954, we ended up in a new development which had a Westbury address but was adjacent to Levitt houses in the backyard. We moved into 86 Murray Drive in the summer of 1954. The house cost $14,000, had three rooms, a basement, no garage, one bathroom, a living room, an entrance foyer and a central hall. Doris decided she was not going back to teaching and we used the money she had built up in the teachers' retirement fund to have a garage built on the side of the property in the back of the house. The driveway extended from the front curb past the rear stairway leading to the kitchen. The driveway had little clearance from the chimney, which was built on the side of the house. Every trip to the garage was an exercise in tight steering.

In 1956, I finally accumulated enough college credits to graduate. The ceremonies were held in the Brooklyn Academy of Music on a very hot evening in June. I had to ask my mother to attend my graduation because Doris was about to give birth to our second child. Karen was born a week later. I could now hang up my diploma as a Bachelor of Electrical Engineering. It didn't make much of an impact on my job. I showed the diploma to the brass at 30 Church Street and their overall reaction was "very nice" and nothing else.

The big problem with living at 86 Murray Drive was a nasty neighbor who lived next door, didn't want Jews in the neighborhood, and made our lives miserable. His daughter even attacked Karen with a baseball bat. After a confrontation, he got belligerent and shot out the light over my garage. I went to the police. After hearing my story the detective informed me that I must be overly paranoid about such incidents. The neighbor was a fraternity lodge brother, and the police had no power to intervene. Another police officer gave me more practical advice and told me to move away. In 1961, we finally found the house that would meet our needs.

Karen's comment:

When I was 4 years old in 1960, I was attacked by a neighbor (a girl) wielding a baseball bat. She wasn't much older than me, taught by her parents that "Jews were bad." Due to a concussion I was briefly hospitalized. I have no memory of the assault. I was made aware when I turned 18 as the statute of limitations for legal action was about to expire. Until recently I made no connection between my father's experience with antisemitism and my own childhood episode. I still have a baseball bat-shaped dent in my head as evidence.

Sid wrote more detailed descriptions about his career than the progress of his kids throughout childhood, adolescence and into adulthood. It was, after all, the "Mad Men" era when mothers bore the brunt of childrearing duties and fathers snapped the Kodak photos. Dad left for work early and got home late. He always showed up for the important milestones. I learned the foxtrot by standing on his feet while he danced (a skill sadly not tapped into as an adult). And he clapped the loudest at every band (Dan) or choral (Karen) performance.

Historical note: Even though the borough of Brooklyn is geographically located on the tip of Long Island, it is considered "the city," along with the neighboring borough of Queens. Long Island is 23 miles wide and 118 miles long, only half a mile from Manhattan Island as the crow flies, and the largest island in the contiguous United States. Residents in the densely populated portions tend to consider the outlying parts of the island a world away. Migration from Brooklyn to the Long Island suburbs took hold in the 1950s. Suburban exodus was driven by bank loans targeted at returning soldiers, referred to generically as "Government Issue (GI) Joes." It was a path for families to raise children in house with yards instead of cramped apartments. There were also organized efforts to frighten people that racial minorities were going to take over the region, triggering "white flight." My father recalled campaigns financed by Fred Trump (father of Donald) where trucks rolled through city streets, men using bullhorns to warn them the neighborhood was doomed. This tactic opened up housing availability and lowered the price for real estate developers to buy old, rundown buildings.

Chapter 12

Suburban Life

Sid:

There was a new development in Old Bethpage, Long Island featuring homes with three bedrooms, two bathrooms, a large kitchen, living room, laundry room, family room, and a garage advertised as holding two cars. The house I selected cost $26,500. We moved into 26 Kingswood Drive in the spring of 1961. The house had a real front porch, a full access attic and a huge basement, all attractive features. We lived in that house for the next 22 years.

In 1961, also, the installation engineering group moved into the new Western Electric headquarters building in downtown New York. It was a brand new 27-story skyscraper with fully air-conditioned offices. I had endured the discomfort of the old rented quarters at 30 Church Street for ten years. The old building was close to the docks where coal burning ships would anchor. The coal dust would enter the office through large windows extended from floor to ceiling. A clean white shirt would have a black ring around the collar by noon. On the hot humid summer days, we would have to cover drawings with paper towels to prevent perspiration from staining the blueprints. The new offices had fluorescent lighting and even new fireproof furniture, as well as modern high-speed elevators. We moved into the ninth floor of 222 Broadway in the summer of 1961.

My life settled into a routine of commuting on the Long Island Railroad and raising the family. At work, I became a specialist in long distance communication equipment and had to do much traveling around the country. As the years went by, the installation engineering organization started to lose its clout and became a subsidiary under the Telephone Sales organization.

Finally, in 1966, a decision was made to dissolve the headquarters organization and transfer the installation engineers to the manufacturing location matching their expertise. For my department, it meant moving to Columbus, Ohio. I had no intention of moving into the factory and wrote a letter to upper management containing a number of reasons why I wished to stay in New York. Their reply was there was no assignment available for me and I would be terminated if I didn't go to Columbus. I held my ground and promised if they kicked me out, I would write to every New York paper and physically picket the headquarters building to show how the company was treating an employee after 25 years of dedicated service. I knew the company would not tolerate that kind of publicity.

They kept up the story there was no job for me right up to the last Friday when the furniture was moved out and I was to lock the doors and hand the keys to the maintenance crew. That afternoon, I found a letter on my desk ordering me to report to the corporate engineering planning organization which was located on the 14th floor of the main AT&T headquarters building at 195 Broadway, a block away. When I reported on the following Monday, the manager wanted to know why I had waited so long to take the job. It had been vacant for three months awaiting an experienced engineer to take on a backlog of special assignments. The company had put a squeeze play on me while they knew this job was available all that time. Well, that's how big corporations work.

The engineering planning group was involved primarily with manufacturing engineering. The job was to work closely with the Bell Laboratories on new developments, determine the potential market for the product, determine the manufacturing technology required, select the manufacturing location, calculate the costs involved and prepare a presentation for the Vice-President, Corporate Engineering, to present to the company Board of Directors to convince them to spend the seed money to bring the new development into production. The job required frequent trips to the manufacturing sites and I became familiar with the facilities needed to produce the product lines.

For the next 15 years, I developed expertise in transmission and data systems, printed wiring board technology, connection systems, and finally, solid state electronic devices. I was directly involved in setting up the first product line to manufacture integrated circuit chips. When I first joined the engineering planning group, I learned the personnel assignments had been rotational, with engineers coming from the plants for a two year stretch at headquarters as part of their training for higher level management positions. I offered a deal to the director to set up a permanent cadre of specialists who would maintain a continuity of experience and skills to make the organization more efficient.

There could be no promotions under this setup but I proposed the salary treatment should be commensurate with the increased value of the specialists to the company. The proposal for a permanent cadre was given one year as a trial and it was still in force when I retired fifteen years later. Although I retained the same title of Senior Engineer for the whole period, I did receive regular salary increases as if I were on the managerial development track. When I retired, I had reached an annual salary of $50,000, which was a fairly high amount for that time.

The children grew up and Doris and I got older. My mother Annie died in 1965 at the age of 78. Doris' sister, Edie, died in 1971 of ovarian cancer. She was only 44 years old. Doris' mother, Fannie, died soon afterward.

Karen went off to Buffalo in 1974 on a college scholarship, went to graduate school in California and eventually developed a career in health care management. Daniel got married in 1978 to Robin Nussbaum and stayed on Long Island. Their son Bradley was born in 1983.

By the time 1981 came around, I was looking forward to collecting forty years of service with the Western Electric Company. However, changes were in the wind. The company was undergoing a reduction in force and an early retirement was presented. Anybody accepting early retirement would receive an incentive bonus of a year's pay in addition to the regular pension. The offer was made in the spring of 1981 and I was officially retired by the end of June. I didn't quite make the full forty years, which would have been in September of that year. As a result, I didn't receive the traditional forty-year anniversary gift. I did get a retirement gift of a Thomas brand mantel clock. Of course, that clock has never kept the right time to this day.

Karen's comment:

Sid's clock drove me crazy for decades. It bonged loudly, didn't keep time, it was tacky. Yet that timepiece was Sid's most treasured possession in his later years, and he carefully wound it every Friday. His possessions shrunk as he shifted into assisted living, but the clock stayed. After Dad died I gave the "vintage" clock to Thomas (aptly named) and Laurie, AirBnB hosts who became my (and Sid's) friends. For some bizarre reason they really like it. A nod to Thomas for suggesting I call this book "Preserving My Inheritance" to keep with the pickle theme. Growing up, I knew Dad spent every day on the Long Island Railroad. I knew he was an engineer. And in the unique way children can put ideas together, I thought he was the engineer running the train. When he took me at age 7 to visit him at his job, I was stunned to discover his workplace was an office and not a caboose.

I treasure the letter I received from Dad in 1985, sympathizing with my need to get eyeglasses. Having my vision corrected wasn't a big deal to me, but he had a lifetime of worry about his own eyesight.

Feb 13, 1985

"Dear Karen, I'm sorry to hear about your need for eyeglasses but you are only joining the family weaknesses. Your mother and I have worn glasses for so long that I can't remember ever having been without them. It's not the worst tragedy in the world. As your mother pointed out, you still have youth, beauty, intelligence and strength of character going for you. To me, you will be our bright and beautiful daughter no matter what kind of glasses you wear. I'm enclosing $200 to cover some of your immediate expenses. Please don't exhaust your savings while at school. Love, Dad."

76

Chapter 13

Retirement in California

Sid:

After one year of retirement in Long Island, we decided to move to Southern California. We had visited there as early as 1978. Karen had received a fellowship to the University of California at Irvine and we had visited her and toured the area. In 1981, we had visited my cousin, Ruth Schunk, in San Diego, and she took us around the area, showing us places where we could live. Private homes were prohibitively expensive but we found a mobile home complex that looked attractive. In 1982, we sold our Old Bethpage home and purchased a mobile home built to my specifications at the New Frontier Mobile Home Park in Santee. The home itself was prefabricated in two halves at the factory and was trucked to the site. The two halves were assembled at the selected lot and a custom built deck and garage were constructed around the living quarters. The home was completely equipped with carpeting and kitchen appliances and was ready for occupancy when the assembly was complete.

We lived in the mobile home park for three years but I wasn't happy with the idea of paying rent on the land while owning the home. A further objection was the discovery there was an easement for a public thoroughfare through the center of the park. In 1985, we learned of a new development of private homes about three miles from the mobile park, being built on the ridges of Rattlesnake Mountain, which was the highest location in Santee. The original developer had died in an airplane crash and the local Crocker Bank had taken over the property when the loan was foreclosed. A brash young developer picked up the property at one-third its value and built one hundred homes on the site. Because he had purchased the property so cheaply, he offered the homes on a minimum of a half-acre lot for a very attractive price. The only twist was he charged a premium for every level above the street, up to the highest ridge of the mountain. The house at the top had a premium of $19,000. I paid a premium of $5,000 for a level slightly below the top ridge. The house cost $124,000.

It was only after I retired I learned the actual cause of my loss of vision in my left eye. When Doris developed glaucoma, we went to a special ophthalmic facility associated with the University Hospital. After the doctor examined me, he told me my eye sockets were of unequal depth, a birth defect. Although the retina and optic nerve in my left eye were not damaged, my brain could not accept an out-of-focus image from one of the eyes, and the signal from the left eye was essentially shut down. Partial sight was restored when I got my first pair of glasses at age 10 and I spent many hours trying to read with the left eye only. Had my eyes been examined and fitted with glasses as a young child, I would have 20/20 vision in both eyes today. In the culture of that time, there was no such thing as preventive pediatric care. When Daniel showed signs of strabismus in one eye, we had him undergo corrective surgery at age seven. Karen appeared to have normal eyesight, and I was thankful for that.

Two years after I retired, the Bell System was broken up as a result of a lawsuit brought on by a small taxi company in Texas wanting a direct connection from their two-way radio into the telephone system. This incredibly complex case was submitted to a totally ignorant jury who had no comprehension of the issues involved. The jury decided in favor of the taxi company and the judge ordered the dissolution of the Bell System. That small taxi company was MCI, which became the second largest communications company in the country. As part of the breakup, the Western Electric Company was dissolved and the remaining portions were absorbed into the parent AT&T company. I was very disheartened by the obliteration of my long-term employer but I did get one unexpected benefit of the move. I was now a retired engineer of AT&T and was eligible for a discount on long distance calls.

The vulnerabilities of age now are taking their toll and I have to consider how many more years of life we both have left. Doris and I are both diabetic, both have arthritis, and both have cardiac problems. Doris had open-heart surgery early in 1995, and underwent eye surgery in August. Her vision is expected to return slowly. I developed an irregular heart rhythm and have learned to live with a condition called atrial fibrillation, which essentially is a reduced efficiency of the heart muscle. I must use an anticoagulant medication for the rest of my life. We manage from day to day, watching the clock to time all our medication and scheduling visits to all the doctors involved in our care. I am very relieved we are fully covered by medical insurance for all of our ailments.

We never developed any really close friends and have to depend on each other for survival. I like living in my own private home but may have to consider a different environment if either of us becomes truly incapacitated. Meanwhile, I want my children to read this story with the hope that it fills in their knowledge of the man they called "Dad."

Karen's comment:

Sid doesn't mention that he actually watched his wife's open heart surgery. Somehow he snuck into the observation suite reserved for visiting doctors, where he got to see the action. Hospital security wasn't as tight those days. Staff assumed he was a professor emeritus. When they realized he was a spouse and not a physician, they politely (with some alarm) escorted him to the waiting room. He considered it "very instructional" to witness the procedure and never considered the emotional aspects. Sid was a wanna-be doctor. He volunteered at the medical school's biomedical engineering department for decades.

Did Sid ever share his writings with Doris, or was it a private journal he only wanted his children to read later? I don't know. I suspect he didn't purposely share it with his wife, despite their close bond. Knowing her history (she read my sixth grade private diary), she may have found it and read some of the early parts. Mom made fun of him disappearing into his man-cave office, late at night. She would call me to say "I never know what he's doing in there." At this point Sid had 29 single-spaced typed pages and realized his autobiography needed technological intervention. It was also at this time I became more involved and visited my parents more often, especially as my awareness of their health problems grew. Starting in January 2010, I decided to capture the nuances of my parents' transition with a personal blog, titled "*Aging Quirky.*"

Sid's parents, Dave and Annie Vogel. Wedding picture, 1910

Annie Vogel, proud U.S. citizen in 1914

Sid's caricature, drawn by a military buddy, 1943

Picnic date with Doris, 1946   *Wedding kiss, 1947*

84

Business man – suit and tie

Western Electric engineering graduates, 1962

Dan, age 5, with a fashion neck tie, 1956

Karen, the baby, with a full diaper, 1956

Sid's typewriter, before he built a computer

When life gave him lemons, Sid planted a lemon tree.
Santee house backyard, 1990

Extension cord curtain, Sid's garage

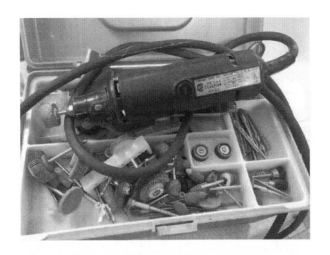

Sid's industrial grinder, used for personal mani-pedi

Graduating to a professional manicure, 2017

Custom cheesecake for the pickle king's birthday, 2014

Sid's grumpy look at Subway, 2015

Devouring imitation New York pizza, 2016

Enjoying fresh latkes with pickles, 2016

Sid in the cockpit for his birthday flight, 2017

Chapter 14

Karen the Writer

My blog was titled *Aging Quirky: Karen's Chronicle*. The description: *"Sharing stories to give you a personal glimpse into the strange dynamics of aging in America."*

The blog was initially only available for a select group of friends going through similar experiences with their own parents. The first post was written before a trial stay at a retirement community in Encinitas, the place where my father ultimately relocated.

Blog Post #1
January 6, 2010: Entering Q-Tip World

For those of you with white-haired elderly parents, or who have met mine, welcome. My folks are both 87, in deteriorating health, stubborn, and smart - a tricky combination for anyone to deal with, but especially for them. I'm the responsible adult-child, ill-equipped to handle geriatric case management, but well-versed in dysfunction (I have New York roots).

As my parents have become more isolated and need more resources (don't ask about the driver's license debacle), moving into a "facility" has become a more attractive option - sort of. They are at least willing to experience a trial stay - senior summer camp, if you will. The catch? Per their request, I have to go with them. My role is to ease their transition. So . . . I will be staying this weekend at a retirement community in my own guest suite, observing the action. I'm journaling due to a self-serving therapeutic need to manage my own anxiety.

Giving credit where credit is due, I thank my parents for their genetic transmission of a fine sense of irony, along with appreciation of the absurd.

Coming soon:

Bargaining, pleading & coercion - dealing with old people;
Irrational moments - stuff you can't make up; and
Social networking, senior-style!

Karen's comment:

While starting the blog, I cajoled their primary care physician at the time (a pediatrician) into signing a California State form to ban my father from driving. For a while Sid had been swerving lanes, bashing poles in parking lots and almost hit a bicyclist. He insisted on a road test and failed twice. Dad blamed the doctor for his loss of independence and never outwardly acknowledged my involvement. He knew how bad his driving had become, his denial of the problem eventually softened.

January 8, 2010: The Prep

I arrived at my parent's house at noon to find them still in their jammies, not packed, fully in the throes of denial. It took only an hour to get them somewhat ready. I had to promise I would rent a van to drive all of Dad's tools to Seattle when/if he moved out. We are still negotiating about the thousands of vacation slides he made over the past 60 years (does anyone want the slides?)

My folks were really excited about getting their hair cut – since the loss of Dad's driver's license (which he only brought up every 10 minutes) they have both become hairy hermits, emerging only to go to doctor appointments. So – blinking in the California sun, we troop off to get shorn. Somehow my father has found a re-creation of a dingy barber shop from the lower east side of NY. He sat in the chair like a king, ordering the young cutter "take more off!" take more off!" The poor guy, I had to sneak in afterwards to give him a big tip. Meanwhile, my mother sat in the lady's version down the street, getting her eyebrows trimmed and demanding they honor 2-year old coupons.

Driving here was uneventful; I had upgraded the car rental to get one with 4 doors so everyone could get in without chiropractic adjustment. Fortunately I brought an emergency supply of bagels for snacking. We arrived at the facility on time – amazing! – and I noticed with relief there is a brewery conveniently located down the street.

January 9, 2010: Beware, All Walkers Look Alike

We were briefly inspected – forms shoved in a drawer without comment (I had spent hours making sure their medical forms/TB tests/etc. were done). Despite bringing enough clothing for a month, somehow my mother forgot her toothbrush – off I went to the local drugstore. Afterwards we all met with our official greeter, assigned to follow Mom and Dad for a week to make sure they didn't steal the silverware.

Dinnertime! At 5 pm, of course. Here is the senior networking part. Would you believe my mother hooked up with a friend from Brooklyn College, where she graduated from in 1942? Yes, the girls looked a little different but they still talk the same. And of course there's Ida, the 90-plus year old fitness queen. Ida walks to the YMCA every day to work out wearing color-coordinated outfits. My mother and Ida used to live near each other about 20 years ago; they became casual friends. At a recent lunchtime visit here, my mother yelled across the room "Ida! I thought you were dead!" Nice.

Dad counted all the guys in the dining room: there were 9. Older men don't last as long as the women. One lady told me "we used to have a table of 14 people who liked to eat together – all the male spouses passed on, so now there are just 7." Another new friend was whispering in my mother's ear "It's not so good here. Come to Room 253 after dinner and I'll dish the dirt." The folks here have their cliques.

We all rushed off (mostly rolled off, in a sea of blue walkers) for the evening entertainment, a piano concert in the lobby. The music was actually quite nice despite the occasional snoring from the attendees. My father loaded up on the free brownies and piled them up on my mother's walker seat – he took not one, not two, but SIX brownies back to their room. He managed to lose one brownie, step on it, mash it into the hallway carpet, and keep moving.

I asked if he intended to eat the brownies – no, he wanted to put them in the mini-fridge just in case he gets hungry in the middle of the night. Upon inspecting their room after 3 hours of use, the bed was piled with clothing, and the bathroom was full of junk. In other words, the hoarding impulse was immediate and the place looked just like their house.

January 20, 2010: Calling the Cops

After trying to reach my parents by phone for 3 days, getting a busy signal at all hours of the day and night, I considered not even my father could be working on the computer that long (he has a dial-up connection, the last one in America). I considered the phone could be off the hook, I considered they could be having a wild party. I considered they could be in big trouble. I tried calling one of their neighbors to no avail. So, doing what every paranoid crime-buster would do, I called the police to investigate. Not 911, as that would be drastic. I called the non-emergency dispatch unit of the local sheriff's department. Figured they were bored anyway. To credit the police, they were responsive, polite and sent an officer out to my folks' house within 20 minutes.

A polite deputy guided Dad to a special police phone to call me and say hello. Mom apparently slept through the whole event. I heard my father telling the officer "well, that's my daughter. She's very thoughtful but such a worry wart." It turns out the town lost all phone and some electrical service for the past 72 hours due to tornado watches, floods and winds. While I know California experiences "weather" I thought it meant a few rain showers. Sometimes you just have to go with your gut. I don't regret sending the coppers out – at least now they have a case record for the next incident, and I can bring them donuts on my next trip.

To bring everything up to date, my parents successfully checked out of their trial stay at the retirement facility and are actually considering moving there. They talked to a real estate agent about putting their house on the market. Mom is recognizing they have to downsize. She cleaned off the kitchen counter – while that may not seem significant, it's a BIG deal. We haven't seen the counter since 1988 due to the piles of expired coupons, pill bottles, old magazines and crusty ketchup packets. I believe the hardest part – acceptance that their current housing situation isn't good - is over. Practical logistics come next. Onward!

March 13, 2010: The Folks Set a Date!

I spent the morning trying to convince my mother she could part with shoes which no longer fit, were popular decades ago, had stacked heels, or only matched glitter outfits. I threw all the shoes in a box and hid them in the car trunk for eventual disposal. I already made one secret run before breakfast to the thrift shop with piles of clothing, most of it size large, never worn. Note that my mother is 4 foot 10, weighs 100 pounds, is quite petite – but these clothes were really good bargains in their time.

We went off for yet another free lunch at the retirement facility -- herring/gefilte fish salad, an acquired taste. Next on the agenda was visiting an apartment held for them since January. We took pictures. We measured counters. We took turns sitting on the shower seat. We discussed how to fit 6 broken vacuum cleaners and hundreds of old bed sheets into a place offering cleaning once a week and free linens.

Maybe it was watching the old family movies last night, maybe it was a growing realization they couldn't rely on their neighbors much longer for trips to the grocery store, maybe it was just the right time -- but they agreed to commit to a move-in date.

Imagine my surprise when my father whipped out his checkbook – even after the facility had waived the deposit and move-in fee – to ensure they had a spot. Much negotiation ensued about the date – the marketing manager wanted April Fool's Day, I was positioning for Mother's Day, my mother asked "Can you hold it until Labor Day? We need some more time." We settled on May 27 as the absolute deadline. Everyone shook hands, I blinked back tears of relief, and immediately went into micro-planning mode to facilitate the transition. If it were up to me, I would hire movers to come tomorrow, with or without the post-it notes.

I brought back the box of shoes from the car trunk for my mother to go through again. Heck, she can keep them all if she wants. Some things I totally understand.

March 15, 2010: Running Low on Bananas

I've lost count of how many trips I've made to supermarkets to stock up on essentials: bananas, mustard, smoked salmon, pickles. My parents are hoarding food in 3 refrigerators – how will they ever downsize to one?

Today's accomplishments: I managed to pack all the photo albums and ship them to Seattle. I went with Dad to the bank to rearrange his accounts and ensure a free safety deposit box at any branch for life. I reinstalled his internet service after he accidentally removed it. I talked to real estate agents and showed them the extension cord curtain in the garage. Only one agent, Valerie, was excellent, sensitive to geriatric issues, and paid attention to detail. For a total of 4 hours, we all learned about plumbing, floods, termites, and other plagues that will deflate the market price. Then we managed to go to dinner, after the frantic daily hunt for the house keys. Dad was frustrated he couldn't find his favorite jacket, and I had a growing dread I stuffed it in one of the donated sacks of clothing. I was on the verge of confessing when it turned up in the bathroom.

Future options include an estate sale, an auction, a painting party, and/or a landscaping intervention. I had previously promised to drive all the tools up to Seattle in a truck. I could rent a van to transport everything not picked over to my friend's house one hour away and hold a giant garage sale. I'll pretend to be on the road for a few days, no one will be the wiser.

May 17, 2010: It was Supposed to be Moving Day

I should have known it wasn't going to be this easy. If my parents don't die peacefully in their sleep, I may consider killing them. No, not really.

To get up to date, a few significant events have transpired. First: my mother went into panic mode about moving to a retirement facility while my father was all gung-ho – a complete reversal of their stance 6 months ago. They cancelled the apartment, got back their deposit, and created a lot of drama. Second: they attempted to get the house ready for sale by hiring a contractor, which was a sobering challenge and only unveiled the tip of the iceberg.

As soon as the wall cracks were repaired, there was a 7.2 earthquake in Mexico which created – you guessed it, more cracks. Mom felt the ground shaking, got dizzy, assumed her diabetes drugs weren't working, and called the doctor to complain about the strength of her prescriptions. Third: Mom switched her primary care physician to someone more inclined to listen to her complaints (but located many miles away, requiring insurer-supplied transportation).

I tried a new tactic – offered to personally take ALL the stuff, so nothing would get dumped in a landfill or another Goodwill bin; it would just be magically transported to my attic in Seattle. Yes, it was a little white lie. Mom's response – "Why would you want all that junk?" This stumped me for a bit (why is she hanging on to 50 years of broken plastic if she knows it's crap – clearly, it's about security and memories, not the things).

Yesterday she told me my father will only accept a community offering 3 bedrooms, 2 bathrooms, large walk-in closets, 3 giant meals a day, etc. Of course the idea of anyone entering their current home to help clean or cook is simply not acceptable.

So where does that leave the story? Well I'm not offering any assistance or opinions for a while. Instead of visiting my parents, I'm going camping with friends in a heated yurt. I'm waiting for the inevitable call about a fall or heart attack. It's not an amusing way to end this post, but this fate is unfortunately their next likely chapter.

Chapter 15

Impasse

Sid: October 2008

Doris and I have both reached the age of 86 and are still bumbling along. We have been looking at retirement centers and have not found them very attractive. The house still requires upkeep maintenance and my energy level has decreased somewhat. Doris has great difficulty in walking and she suffers from a condition called organic volvulus which twists her stomach while she is eating. This requires her to eat small meals at regular intervals during the day. It is difficult to plan meals to meet both of our needs but we manage to get through the day without starving.

I have informed the crew at the hospital I shall be retiring from my volunteer work at the end of this year after 24 years of service. I would have liked to complete 25 tears but Doris is firm in my leaving as soon as possible. I took two months out to care for her after she had an accident while falling on the concrete walking down the driveway to pick up the mail. I had warned her about her unsteady balance on firm surfaces but she ignored the risk. She broke her wrist this time. She fell the same way last year but managed to get away without breaking anything. She still has to wear a brace on her arm during the day. Our health insurance allows us to use a family doctor whose office is only ten minutes away from our home. We pay a heavy monthly premium for our health care, and we have a short window to make any plans for 2009.

Sid: May 2010

We are approaching the age of 88. I have given up my driving license and sold the car to a neighbor. He takes me shopping once a week and we manage to survive with that service. We have been looking at retirement villages and none of them meet our requirements. They all have advantages and disadvantages. We did like the food available at a place sponsored by the Jewish Federation. The only apartment with two bathrooms was a two room setup with a bedroom and a living room and a sink and a refrigerator in the living room. No actual kitchen. We got an offer of waiving the so-called community fee of $3,000 if we could move in by May 27. I put down a deposit hoping to sell the house quickly but it became evident we couldn't make that date and my deposit was returned.

We did try to make the house saleable by spending $5,000 to correct defects which included replacing a section of the wall in the front bedroom and removing the fiberglass panels covering the front entrance. Some tiles in the roof had to be removed to correct the pitch of the drainage path and were later replaced. Minor plumbing was done along with painting in the kitchen and dining area. We are trying to unload as much as we can to get rid of the clutter drowning every room. It is a burdensome task and will take a long time to clear the house. Meanwhile, there are boxes everywhere full of stuff to be reviewed for discard. Our health is declining but our spirits are still upbeat. Let's hope the next addendum will not be written by Karen announcing our demise.

Karen:

September 16, 2010: Random Tidbits

My father, now traveling in cars as a passenger, vehemently argues with the GPS voice when it gives directions. He thinks it's my mother trying to tell him when to turn, and "Dammit, that's not the best way to get there!"

My mother has to get unpleasant catheters inserted due to chronic urinary infections, and the nurses don't always aim so well. She is using a Sharpie marker on her privates to draw an arrow with the suggested path.

No more talk of moving out of the house. At least in Mom's case, she is probably no longer eligible for an independent living situation and would have to go straight to assisted living. The wait continues for the inevitable crisis and I jump when the phone rings late at night.

February 11, 2011: Calling in the Troops

My folks have a new doctor, a new insurance company and a new case manager – and in one of life's strange coincidences, I know her. Vivian worked at a health plan which was a client from my phase in health insurance account management.

I feel like I've been screaming "fire" in a crowded theatre and someone finally heard me. Vivian spent 90 minutes talking to my mother. She spent an hour talking with me. She read everything I sent her, and she follows up within minutes. She is badgering the doctor's office to get referrals processed, she is recommending a home health nurse twice a week, she is sending a social worker once a month, and she is assigning the same driver to transport them to medical appointments for consistency. She is strongly advocating they reconsider the move to the retirement community. She thinks my mother is smart rather than annoying. Relief! Not that I expect miracles, but at least someone else is monitoring the mess.

April 4, 2011: Re-Entry to Reality

My cell phone just rang with a mystery San Diego area code. I answered it to find my parents' neighbor informing me how fire trucks are all over their house and it looks chaotic. My brain goes into "Okay, this is the inevitable crisis, I knew this was coming, at least it didn't happen while I was out of the country." I profusely thank her, then call my mother to find out their smoke alarm doesn't work properly and they're getting an inspection. She's fine, he's fine, and they are still hiding out in suburban hell, refusing care and relocation.

Rewind: the back story. There was a coupon for a free alarm installation -- but Mom apparently called the wrong number and got emergency response instead. And hey, it was a slow day so the firemen spent a few hours fixing things. The crew noted their address for future visits -- sensing in all likelihood they would be returning soon.

February 20, 2012: To Laugh or Cry – Part 1

Well it's time to check on the supply of crusty ketchup packets, so I'm heading down to Santee in a few days. Also, my father is having hernia surgery, which is normally minor but in an 89-year old, not so simple. My brother has flown in from New York, and his anxiety is ramping up. Dan's role is to provide transit for errands, deposit Dad at the hospital, and remember to pick him up. Then he leaves town and I show up a few hours afterwards. Unfortunately, the rental car company flaked out and he asked me to assist. My first mistake: I overreacted. I got hold of a supervisor, I threw a hissy fit about elderly folks at risk, I called the neighbors. Ultimately it worked out. I also asked my 29-year old nephew to step up and be the adult in the family, since the rest of us are bad at it.

Mistake #2: I checked back today to find out my brother tried to get rid of the six non-working vacuum cleaners and bought a new one from the local Walmart. What a snafu. Dad insisted a little more duct tape would solve the problem, refusing to open the new ecologically sensitive unit, and saying no one could see the dust anyway. Especially my mother, who is losing her sight in her remaining good eye, freaking out with anxiety attacks, and insisting my father is trying to kill her. I'm thinking there isn't room for any more electrical cords to be used as curtains; maybe Dad got the hernia from trying to relocate them.

There's a conference call on Wednesday with my parents, the case manager, the social worker, me, my brother, and my cousin Mike, who is the only semi-balanced one in the extended family. I set it up as an intervention to try to get some home care, meal delivery, and miscellaneous resources in place. I don't expect miracles.

I got a massage this afternoon, which was first smart thing I've done lately. For some strange reason, during the massage I thought a lot about my maternal grandmother, who died when I was 15. She's trying to tell me something important, but I don't know what it is.

February 25, 2012: To Laugh or Cry – Part 2

The family conference call took place and was reasonably successful. Eight of us took turns explaining our perspective about how aging sucks; my nephew being the most coherent. Meals on Wheels service starts on Monday 3 times per week. Maybe Dad will let them past the front door since it's easier than him trying to cook. Mom is embarrassed by having this service since it's meant for low income people.

I'm now in San Diego, staying in a private room at a youth hostel close to Ocean Beach, complete with aging surfers, yogurt smoothies, and happy dogs running on the sand. The hostel has a giant lizard basking in the common area, which calms me. I'm sleeping here for a few days. It's a friendly and clean place, quiet and mellow.

I drive to my parents' house each day at 11 am, which is when they wake up. They live in a soul-less suburb with giant RVs and many fast food choices. My mother is going deaf and blind, yelling at my father constantly. My father sleeps a lot, partly from being on Vicodin after his recent surgery and partly to escape my mother. I drove him 20 miles today to get ink cartridge refills for his ancient printer, just so he could get a break.

I have been trying to scrub decades of dirt and dust, with minimal success. Since my brother tried to vacuum last week, I chose other challenges. The toilet broke this morning – according to my father, because my mother plugs it up with paper. According to my mother, because my father keeps forgetting to throw bleach into it to kill tree roots. They keep each other alive by goading each other. Their daily highlight is getting the mail to peruse coupons for deals they will never use.

I was keeping it together, stoically running errands and pretty much ignoring their symbiotic routine. Then I talked to the neighbor who drives Dad to the grocery store each week. She told me he teases her about coloring her hair, telling her "You should let it go silver like my daughter, who is proud and beautiful." Then I lost it, because he would never directly give that kind of compliment to me. That nice lady had no idea why I ran out of her living room.

I tried to go swimming to revert back to the womb, however the local pool was closed. My sanity was saved by having dinner with a friend who made me drink lots of wine. Tomorrow morning I'm going to walk the ocean pier to clear my head, drive east, and start the fun all over again.

February 27, 2012: To Laugh or Cry – Part 3

Yesterday was a 7-hour marathon of laundry. The bed linens fell apart when I removed them. The washer's spin cycle doesn't work, requiring each sopping load to go through the dryer 3 times. I saw things which may scar me for life. Since my mother cleaned up my shit 55 years ago, I returned the favor. Enough said.

Today was a series of trips going back and forth, including a doctor visit to find out my mother has a bad eye infection, but isn't really going blind - yet. She complained loudly in the waiting room about health care and Republicans, and when there was no response, she complained about apathetic voters.

I took advantage of my father's woozy state on pain drugs to strike a deal. If he would let me take away his ancient, heavy vacuum cleaner, I would drive him to Costco to get a decent one, and then I would return the flimsy one my brother bought last week, He held out for Fry's Electronics, his former sanctuary. I tried to throw in 2 of 3 plugged up electric brooms. He offered up a broken sponge mop. As a skilled negotiator, I knew when to fold.

I frantically stuffed every broken appliance I could find into the rental car while Dad was in the bathroom, plus an assortment of crumpled garden hoses. Just like that old TV show where people grabbed as many items as possible in their shopping carts. I was so excited I forgot to close the car door and things started falling out as I drove down the street. I found the electronics recycling center, and quickly unloaded everything while his head was down.

Then, in a sudden rainstorm, off we went 20 miles away to Fry's Electronics. As we pondered the array of choices, a friendly shopper commented "Hey, you know you can get these 2 models for half price at a local discount store in Santee – plus I have a 25% off coupon you can use." This guy told me he lived in Arizona, was visiting his elderly mother in Santee, and was running around trying to make her happy. Kindred spirits. Anyway, Dad immediately insisted we drive all the way back home in rush hour traffic, where he gleefully bought a vacuum that was a DEAL. It's unlikely he will ever take it out of the box.

P.S. My rental car is full of clumps of dirt; ironically I have no way to clean it.

August 30, 2012: So Many Layers

I'm back in San Diego again. Mom got a vitrectomy on her eye this morning, specialized surgery to clear up the debris floating around from prior botched attempts. A strange historical moment: the Scripps Mercy admitting nurse handing my 90-year old mother a Fujitsu tablet and asking her to tap consent into the Electronic

108

Medical Record system. Mom's first high tech experience. I had faith in her surgeon's attention to detail because he noticed my many bruises and asked if I was okay (I fell off a ladder – my garage paint looks good, I don't.)

Today is Mom's actual birthday. After surgery was over, the medical staff decorated her with a giant banner like a beauty queen; I promptly posted the picture on Facebook to rave reviews. Considering all the things that might have gone wrong, the procedure was quite the success. We celebrated with takeout deli and cheesecake, which was not at all diabetic-compliant.

Afterwards, I took advantage of my mother's lack of sight and my father's exhaustion to throw out rotting fruit, stale Halloween candy and assorted artifacts. I found overripe bananas explode when disturbed. I tossed hundreds of magazines in the recycle bin and discovered the mystery cache of soda cans my father was planning to turn in for a reward. After ants started to crawl up my legs, I needed a sanity break at Santee's newest hip hideout – the local microbrewery. It's 5 minutes away, it has decent beer, but alas, no WiFi. I'm back sitting in a lawn chair on the driveway, hacking into the neighbor's connection. I bought my father a year's supply of kitchen garbage bags, which was an exciting product discovery – he's been taping together plastic grocery sacks for decades. For his 90th birthday this Sunday, Hefty bags might be his present.

Another action-packed day is planned for tomorrow with appointments and errands. I am determined to eliminate the rusty lawn furniture in the back yard, wish me luck.

September 1, 2012: So Many Surprises

Here are some of the things that went into a dump truck early this morning: hospital intravenous poles (formerly used to hold up the garage door when it broke), moldy suitcases, ripped lawn chairs, typewriters, tripods, rusty microwave ovens, file cabinets, a large steel desk, aluminum milk crates, fans, heaters, kitchen chairs that lost their legs, and a never-used pith helmet. I told my father I paid the guy $100 to haul it all away; it was actually $200. My mother was still sulking and stayed in bed, screeching "Don't let her get away with this!"

My father ambled out to meet all the neighbors who showed up to try to take his tools – nice, middle-aged guys I had never met until today. They saw the open garage with treasures spilling out, and the giant truck, and they must have figured everyone finally died and it was time for plunder. Now while I do consider poisoning my parents while they sleep, I haven't acted on it. The only stuff I actually want to keep is Dad's tools – there are at least 2 men I know who have been salivating over the tool stash for years. So I grabbed back the ancient hammers and redirected the guys to the ample supply of light bulbs.

After the truck groaned up the hill, I took a long shower and left for the rest of the day, with a stop at Goodwill to offload a broken record player and thousands of vacation slides. I saw parts of coastal San Diego I had never visited, even though I lived here for a while, and appreciated the views and the sunny breeze. I pondered how my parents are going senile in different ways – he is becoming forgetful and transient, she is bitter and angry – not with me, I recognize. She is hostile about aging and losing her mental grip, and who can blame her?

I went to yet another bar – the hunt for a wireless connection is turning me into a lush – and found a garbage bin to dump the many expired pill bottles I rounded up last night. Old drugs are supposed to be disposed to a safe place, I know, but it was either the bin or flushing them down the toilet, and I don't trust their plumbing.

110

Chapter 16

Crisis and Relocation

Karen:

August 25, 2013: Obituary for Mom

Doris Reger Vogel, beloved wife of Sidney and mother of Dan and Karen, was born August 30, 1922 and died August 23, 2013 in Santee CA. Doris was born in Brooklyn NY, pursued a college degree at a time when it wasn't typical, and became a teacher. She met Sidney at age 24 while on vacation in New Hampshire. It was love at first sight: he asked her on a hike, she ruined her shoes, and agreed to marry him 2 weeks later. They were best friends for 66 years of marriage.

Doris, or "Dottie" as she was known to a special few, loved cats, birds, books, community theatre, and making trouble. She is survived by Sidney, her children, her daughter-in-law Robin, and her grandson Brad. She is now at peace with her brother Charlie and sister Edie, who she both lost many decades ago. Her body was donated to the UCSD School of Medicine for research. Doris had a delightful sense of humor and balanced perspective that touched many friends; she will be missed.

Sid: August 2013

Doris had steadily declined to the point where I knew she couldn't fight much longer. She had become so weak she couldn't press the TV remote buttons. On August 23, the nurse had come to the house for her regular checkup. Doris complained she was too tired to get out of bed. The nurse helped her to walk to the recliner. She fell asleep as soon as she settled in the chair. I was making some food for her in the kitchen when the nurse announced she had stopped breathing. She then checked that her heart had stopped. We called 911 and the crew was doing everything they had to restore her heart. They were about to give up when they detected a faint irregular heartbeat. She was rushed over to emergency care at Grossmont Hospital where they worked on her until it was hopeless. The doctor told me her brain had been without blood for too long to keep her alive.

I agreed to their stopping all efforts. In accordance with our contract with the UCSD body donation program, I called them to take her body. I got a nice letter from them saying her organs probably had saved more than one person's life.

Karen's comment:

I recently attended the University of California San Diego School of Medicine's annual memorial ceremony to honor both my mother and father. First year medical and pharmacy students performed music and spoke to the families about how training with cadavers helps them become better, more compassionate physicians. Each body is studied as an anatomy teaching tool; each deceased person impacts hundreds of lives. In this way, Sid really did become a doctor like he wanted.

My parents died a little more than 5 years apart. Things were so hectic when Mom passed that no one was able to attend the ceremony for her. After each year's anatomy module at the medical school, cremated remains are sent by boat out to the Pacific Ocean. A sculpture with all of the donor names is being built nearby at the La Jolla bluffs where my folks used to enjoy watching sea birds. I'll come back to say hello.

Sid and Doris's bond was special, and although I'm not religious, I believe they are together again. To quote Fredrik Backman, "He was a man of black and white. And she was color. All the color he had."

September 8, 2013: The Week After

Exactly one week after my mother died, my father became suddenly ill and started bleeding with what appeared to be a urinary tract infection (UTI). His scheduled eye surgery went on hold and I rushed him to his primary care doctor. Despite pain killers and drugs, it got worse and we went back a second time that day. The doctor sent us home again – a sloppy mistake.

I wound up coordinating an emergency complete with blood clots, vomiting and watching my father struggle in pain. I had never seen him cry and I was petrified. When I briefly left him alone for some privacy on the toilet, he fell grabbing the shower door for support, it smashed and I rushed in to catch him and clean him up. Afterwards, I screamed at my dead mother she couldn't have him yet, I pleaded with her that it wasn't his time. Mom used to get frequent UTIs and complained he didn't understand how awful it was. Well now he certainly understood. Paramedics ultimately rushed him into the Emergency Room the next morning as my brother showed up on the doorstep, straight from a 6-hour flight from New York.

Dad spent 5 days in the hospital attached to a catheter. He spent birthday #91 there with strawberry cake, flirted with the nurses, told me he loved me very much and thanked me for saving his life. I have never had that kind of poignant connection

113

with him in 57 years, or frankly with anyone. He apologized to my brother for being rough on him all his life. It has never been easy for my father to express himself. Now he tells his children every day that he appreciates us. What a tremendous gift.

While Dad recovered that week, my brother and I cleaned out 28 years of household dirt, tattered clothing and broken furniture. It was hard work. However, we made time for laughter throughout many "trash and dash" runs to parking lot dumpsters. We have always had different personalities and styles, but we mutually scaled an emotional fence to support each other.

After Dad's discharge, his first request was to go to the barber – he wanted a short military buzz cut for the past 40 years and my mother would never let him do it. He looks fantastic.

What's ahead is a difficult conversation. An apartment is being held at the same independent living facility was chosen 3 years ago by my mother. While Dad is coming to his own conclusion relocation is logical, actually moving is a whole other matter. I'll be traveling back and forth to assist with the next round of medical care. I understand Dad may die soon due to the impact of losing his spouse and his caretaker role; it's what usually happens in these situations. However if I can facilitate a final happy chapter for that man, I'm going to try my best. He deserves a vacation.

I'm a little worried about my sanity these days, and my anger at my mother. I know I will go through stages of depression and grieving and ultimately, acceptance. I'm trying to take care of myself. David Sedaris, who writes delightful books about angst, declares life is symbolically a four-burner stove: there is one burner each for family, friends, health and work. In order to be successful you have to cut off one of your burners. In order to be really successful, you have to cut off two. I need to pick my burners.

October 1, 2013: The Month After

This morning I drove Dad to the retirement community where he will now make his home. He aced his pseudo-interview, which wasn't easy. He had to walk all over the place, on his own power, with fuzzy vision, wobbly legs, and shortness of breath. He demonstrated his mental agility by informing the director he wouldn't tolerate smokers or Republicans. He offered to fix all the ladies' broken jewelry. When he signed all the forms, he smiled. I allowed myself to cry a bit, hiding in the lobby bathroom. I suppose the stress had to leak out sooner or later.

We went into the dining room for free lunch. Sid's rating: "Not so wonderful. The rye bread could be fresher." I pulled myself together until Ida, the 97-year old powerhouse who still jogs, yelled across the table "Where's your mother?" Ida had been my mother's buddy for 30 years when they both lived in eastern San Diego, and had recommended the facility. When I responded my Mom died, the room went silent, and I started crying again, this time in public. Well, Ida would have none of that, she took me aside and told me to keep walking through life, one step at a time, and that was THAT. When I asked her to help my father get oriented, her loud response was "What, do I look like an official greeter? He's fine. He'll make friends. I'm busy." Then I started laughing, and everyone in the dining room laughed with me.

My brother and I are now going back and forth on cross-country shifts -- cleaning, hiring movers, changing bank accounts. I bought Dad a new recliner chair that doesn't have broken springs and Dan bought a laptop so Dad can leave his rusty dial-up modem behind. I'm tutoring my father to be patient with his healing by reminding him he's always been a tough old bird. He's gradually allowing himself to be happy again. I was granted a leave of absence from work – my job was one of life's stovetop burners put on simmer.

I hope to report a successful move coming up. I have my own building access entry card and I may just hide out there during Seattle's rainy season. A sunny beach is 5 minutes away. And I'm not so picky about the rye bread.

October 25, 2013: Sid's Time to Shine

This is a chapter with a happy ending. It's been an emotional and exhausting week. With a 60-day self-imposed timeline after my mother's death, my father moved on day 59. The apartment he wanted was held for him. The moving truck showed up on time and nothing in the load broke. When Dad entered the lobby of his new residence, Ida was waiting there to welcome him, grinning madly. I got to see the look of pleasure and amazement on Dad's face when he realized I re-created his home, albeit on a smaller scale, down to the pictures on his refrigerator and shelves above his desk (minus the garage full of tools).

Sid is making friends, he's learning how to use high-speed internet, he signed up for a group outing to see community theatre. He has new doctors and is slowly recovering from the infections and surgeries over the last month. Blue haired ladies are flirting with him. He chatted with the maintenance crew to make sure they knew he was supervising their work. He stole food from the dining room by sneaking rolls into his sweatshirt. He's finally safe.

Chapter 17

Settling In

Karen:

November 13, 2013: Priceless Moments

Dad has been in his new home for 3 weeks now, and he's enjoying himself.

Highlights:

Sid signed up for arthritis water class 3 times a week, which was overly ambitious. After the first pool session he was bushed, telling everyone in his path "Those little old ladies kicked my macho butt."

My cousin Marian flew down from Seattle so we could coordinate efforts to hold a massive estate sale. Spanish-speaking families swarmed the house, delighted over the bargains. Everyone received a fluorescent light bulb for coming. The giant 70 pound television was offered for free to the first guy who could lift it. My parents' ancient bed was carted off in a truck to Tijuana. The sale was a huge success. We delivered $300 cash to Sid, expecting he would chuckle and tell us to keep the money for our hard work. No, he stashed all the bills in his wallet and said "Good job!"

Sid's fancy retirement clock got cleaned and repaired. The clock now chimes constantly, driving me nuts, however he's thrilled. Of course it still doesn't keep time accurately, it's usually 3 minutes off - we're going to get it fixed one day.

I shipped home the one piece of furniture I have always liked, a chipped and weary old-fashioned secretary desk with cubbyholes. It turns out it belonged to my great grandmother and it's been in the family since the early days of Brooklyn. I almost had it carted it off to a donation center since it's not worth much money, but changed my mind. The desk arrived with no further damage, and fits into my house like it's been here forever. I'm restoring the desk to its former grandeur by painting it bright red.

I asked Dad to update his life story. I brought a tape recorder since his fingers are gnarled with arthritis; it's harder now for him to type. When I asked him what he would most like to share, he handed me 3 "addenda," the most recent one written a few days ago. He had already summarized his current situation, with no self-pity, on his new laptop. What a wonderful gift; it softens the chaos and pain of the past year. I'm so proud of him.

January 21, 2014: House For Sale

Think about it from the house's perspective. After 28 years of grime, piles of expired coupons and broken patio furniture, it must feel good to finally get cleaned up. Over the past 3 months, walls were painted, windows were washed, and new carpet was installed. Almost immediately the low ball investors – also known as bottom feeders – started calling. Next will be the looky-loo neighbors. After that the brokers arrive – and then maybe actual prospective buyers will come around. I was so happy to drive away for the very last time. I thought about sending a note to the City of Santee, thanking them for their wide diversity of trash bins, my favorite being Walgreens and the YMCA.

Dad wanted to see pictures of his restored house – except for the garage. He couldn't bear to alter the memory of his treasured man-cave. I understand. He's doing fine. Our visits are now a delightful mix of errands, doctor visits and scenic diversions while we discover local restaurants. We enjoy each other's company, and he is smiling again. That's more real than any real estate.

February 10, 2014: Moving On

My parents' house was grabbed within a week by a local couple with cash. A whopper surprise at the last minute was the request for brand new copper plumbing. Ironic since other than an occasional leaky toilet, plumbing was the only thing not broken. I walked away from the offer and said goodbye. Of course they came back a day later with "Never mind." Trying to take advantage of my 91-year old father wasn't nice; I feel vindicated. Plus little did they realize how well Sid knew his pipes.

Dad is kind of sad, he loved his house. He choked up when I congratulated him, so I'm laying low on the "yahoo" tone. By his request, the realtor took my father to Subway for a $5 hoagie after all the papers were notarized. After all, there's no point in wasting money.

Sid: November 2013

Karen and Dan are taking care of emptying the Santee house and making it marketable. We put the house in the hands of a real estate agent whom we know would try hard to sell it. Karen has taken leave from her job to get me settled. Dan and his friend Scott worked hard to empty the house contents. Karen and her cousin Marian conducted a garage sale to sell my amazing collection of stuff. They came back to me with $300 which I promptly pocketed.

Karen's comment:

The perfect storm hit in early 2014: midlife crisis, career dissatisfaction and rapidly deteriorating parents. I realized I could use my training, skills and energy in a different way. I had joked to

119

friends about using my health insurance powers for good rather than evil, but knew it could be true. I understood the jargon and how to access the back doors.

More importantly, I had an ideal experiment in action: my father. After my mother died, Dad needed support in a brand new way. Now Sid looked to me for advice and our parent-child roles were reversed. My professional identity changed to an independent patient advocate, specializing in insurance issues and support for baby boomers with aging parents. Dad was always client number one, which he regularly reminded me.

Chapter 18

Doctors and Parties

Sid: July 4, 2014

Everyone here celebrated the holiday with a special party held in the outside paved courtyard. Speeches, music and a holiday lunch for everybody. I enjoyed the party immensely and had to take two antacid tablets to recuperate. So far, everything looks good for the immediate future.

My health care includes treatment at the onsite therapy center to treat my back pain. The treatment includes a lot of stretching and muscle stimulation with applied heat and electrical pulse stimulation. The session ends with every bone in my body aching. The therapist insists I will improve in time. Karen convinced me to buy a pair of hearing aids but they don't work out too well. I might return them and continue to hear with my remaining capacity.

Karen plans to terminate her job soon. She is tired of constant air travel every week. She has been able to build up sufficient funds to keep going for some time. She is considering working as a consultant with the case manager who handled Doris until her death in 2013. With a whole new generation of baby boomers approaching retirement and applying for Medicare, there will be a massive need for health care management. Meanwhile, she is free to visit me more often. I am enjoying life as she selects places to provide adventure.

Sid: October 2014

Karen has arranged to have me see a dentist after years of neglecting my teeth. The last few years of caring for Doris before her death occupied my time completely. I will not have insurance for the dental work but it will be necessary to have it done to save my remaining teeth. I will have to see a dermatologist also to treat all the skin lesions that have shown up on my scalp and face over the years.

I was having difficulty reading and finally decided to have cataract surgery. I had the first procedure for the right eye done in April while Doris was still alive. It went so well and healed so quickly I scheduled the second procedure for the left eye. It has taken much longer for the left eye to heal. A thorough examination detected a slight bump in the left retina. I have to see a retina specialist and get a clean report before my new ophthalmologist will prescribe new glasses. Meanwhile, I have no use for my existing glasses and everything is still a little fuzzy.

So far, my general health is good, with blood pressure and blood glucose still fairly good under medical and insulin control. My legs are showing improvement in strength and my overall status could be called good.

Sid: January 20, 2015

We had a nice New Year's Party. Dinner that day was lamb chops, a luxury served once a year. Gambling tables were set up as well as an open bar. Champagne was served to all tables. My date was Ida, a 99 year old ball of energy. I am trying to maintain an exercise program set up for me at the fitness center. A few people have died and have been replaced from the waiting list. I try to meet the newcomers and help them until they get the grand tour and personality interview.

I am getting to know the different types of people who come to this facility. At least half of the very old ladies have been living here for as long as eleven years. All of them have run out of money except for their Social Security payments. Nobody is thrown out. They are subsidized from donations from fund raising affairs and contributions from wealthy Jewish families. Another group of residents are relatively young, in the mid-eighties. They have sufficient resources to cover the cost of paying rent of sixty thousand dollars a year.

I have set aside money from the sale of the house to cover rent for three years. If I am still alive after three years, I will have to cash in some of the dividends from my investments.

I will be filing taxes as a single person for the first time. Fortunately, Karen located an AARP advisor at the library who could fill out my forms with the data I had prepared. I was surprised how much I owed. After years of doing all the paperwork myself, all I have to do now is sign my name on the check.

Karen:

March 4, 2015: Taxes, Death and other Certainties

With a nod to Ben Franklin's famous quote, tax season is the universal equalizing experience. After badgering Dad for oh, about 10 years, he finally agreed to have a trained expert do his tax returns. Since AARP sponsors a free consulting service for seniors at the local library, we went there for what I thought would be a quick chat. I gathered every possible piece of paper in his apartment that said 1099 or DIV or "important for your taxes." To his credit, he had attempted to calculate everything on an Excel spreadsheet. However, as we found out today, it's essential to enter commas, not periods – for instance, the amount of $34,000 is different from $34.00.

We got a lucky break with the tax specialist. Rinke is a nice Jewish girl originally from New York, and her own mother lived at Dad's retirement village for 21 years. She calmly organized the multiple copies of the same statements, the mutilated records, and the documents with food stains. She asked Sid what his former profession was, he said "engineer," she smiled and responded "Oh I could tell." She plugged all the data into the government software, muttering a bit, and told us there was a glitch. The computer kept trying to add my mother. I explained Mom periodically shows up to mess with us; she probably wanted a piece of the action. Did the tax lady think this was nuts? Not at all. She shared that her dead mother frequently turns the lights on and off in her home.

Two and a half hours later, we had final results quite shocking to me, but Dad took it all in stride. He still has money in the bank to pay his bills for at least a year. After a recovery nap, off we went to a Purim celebration to have kosher cocktails and rattle

124

noisemakers. I already did my own taxes with TurboTax; now I can spend more time with my father. That's a life refund, better than anything from the IRS.

Chapter 19

Father-Daughter Teamwork

Karen:

July 18, 2014: Shifting Gears

I'm now officially unemployed, able to spend more time with Dad. Caregiving over the last 3 days was a roller coaster. Dad has been receiving physical therapy and making progress with his leg strength, however it leaves him exhausted. So yesterday morning when I found him shaking with confusion, unable to insert his dental bridge, shoes on wrong feet, hearing aid lost, I was alarmed. Somehow he rallied. I stuffed a banana in his mouth and off we went to back pain specialists. When he had 2 helpings at the ice cream social later in the day, I knew he was back on track.

Although Sid's memory is fraying and his body is declining, his sense of humor is intact. I found out his childhood nickname was "Ninny", due to being the baby of his family. We went to the beach to watch the waves, then Costco for hot dogs (extra sauerkraut), and then popped into the infamous Thursday happy hour at his community, where everyone sings. During happy hour I scheduled 3 MRIs and an echocardiogram. I drank a mystery cocktail which had a weird effect of seeing my mother's face on all the ladies. Her ghost still appears at odd times, like when I was folding Dad's laundry last night. She was chuckling about my female servitude.

September 7, 2014: Happy Birthday #92

Highlights from my trip this week:

Packing 7 elderly folks into a rental van (10 minutes), fastening their seat belts (20 minutes), driving through rush hour traffic with everyone offering advice (45 minutes).

Eating deli for Sid's 92nd birthday (20 minutes, the same amount of time as the seatbelts).

Seeing Dad's expression when he was served surprise cake with a pickle-man cartoon painted on top.

Having special friends, including Cindy and Marc, share in the celebration.

Thinking back to a year ago: Sid in the hospital, grieving over my mother, very sick and unsure of his future. We're all in a much better place now.

The morning after the big dinner, we visited Dad's geriatrician for a checkup. I figured with all the binging, Sid's blood pressure would be high and his farts bountiful. Amazingly, the tests were fine. For our family conference, we discussed pastry nuances. The doctor then showed me the results of an echogram, done to analyze Sid's level of cardiac stress. He took me aside, pointing to one high indicator.

> "That's his broken heart. He misses your mom. You've done a great job keeping him healthy and safe. Now you have another assignment. Teach your father how to focus on laughter, continue to have fun together."

I was stunned by his sensitivity and wisdom. And I will absolutely follow doctor's orders.

October 22, 2014: Behind That Smile

Lest anyone think it's all fun hanging out with Dad, consider today's 6 hour dental marathon. It started with me pestering him a few months ago to get his teeth cleaned, realizing he had other priorities over the past 2 years, such as dealing with relocation, depression and death. We had worked through the list of body parts needing repair, and now it was time to focus on oral hygiene. I found a skilled and sensitive (and expensive) dentist who quickly moved beyond flossing to fillings. When he started digging around the cavities he decided there was so much decay a root canal was needed. Off we went to an expert (and expensive) endodontist across the street.

I now realize what's worse than getting a root canal, since I've had a few of my own. What's worse is listening to a root canal being performed on your 92-year old father. Sid did fine. I was a nervous wreck. Actually I was amazed he declined to watch the procedure on the camera screen. He used to enjoy watching my mother's heart surgeries by pretending to be on hospital staff (he actually got into the operating theatre viewing room).

Dad got frozen yogurt as a reward for surviving the torture, and for dinner we had Jewish penicillin: chicken noodle soup. We reviewed all the discounts pursued, making the experience more worthwhile: senior discount, birthday discount, military discount, cash discount (since he doesn't have dental insurance, which wouldn't have helped much). He saved a few hundred dollars due to my creative negotiations. More important, he can keep doing what he does best: eating.

128

November 5, 2014: Mind-Body Connection

Recall I had homework from my father's physician to make sure he had fun, to help him recover from grief and loss. I complied. Along with 8 medical and dental appointments over the past month, we've had lots of trips to the ocean, the desert, the theatre, the deli, and most valued by Sid – Harbor Freight Tools and GTM Discount Store. He now walks 6 laps around his courtyard nearly every day.

Today's exam included an EKG, following up on expected yet troubling indicators for his heart function. The doctor looked up from the graphs and spikes to look directly first at my father, then at me.

> "Your cardiac output has improved remarkably. It's changed by 40%, and this is way more progress than I expected. What have you two been up to?"

I beamed. Sid took it all in stride, and gave me all the credit for his enhanced outlook. The doctor corrected him to emphasize we both deserved credit. He talked about positive attitude and the ability of the human body to respond to laughter and optimism. He produced his prescription pad to write a prescription for local pizza - "no anchovies allowed, too much salt" - with unlimited refills.

The doctor finished our visit with practical tips about how to turn daily struggles of aging into affirmations. When my father complained his left eye didn't work as well as his right despite all the surgeries, the doctor stated "Well then wink and keep that eye shut!"

We drove home along the beach in the fading sunset, which Dad pronounced as "murky" and I considered beautiful. He's got more work to do on that optimism.

Chapter 20

Showers are Dangerous, Part I

Karen:

May 2, 2015: A Horrible Week

Dad slipped in the bathroom 5 days ago and lay bleeding and injured on the floor for 14 hours. He couldn't reach the call button and he had removed his safety pendant for the shower. He wasn't able to answer his phone or door; eventually a housekeeper heard him yelling and he was rescued. He is physically damaged but mentally alert, and will hopefully respond to intense therapy. The rehab unit is located next door to his regular building - there was one bed available which was held for him.

Moments that will stick with me for a long time:

The treating physician at Scripps Hospital asking if he could text me photos of Dad's battered face to consult to make sure the swelling was related to skin cancer treatment and not the fall – versus Dad's local specialist when I tried to text him, snorting "I don't do tele-dermatology, honey."

Dad's friend Shirley taking me into a hallway to press ziplock baggies and rubber bands into my hands, her caring effort to keep my father safe in the shower.

Rushing into Dad's room with a box full of Costco hot dogs and sauerkraut to find 3 nutritionists discussing his dietary preferences and their recommendations for a healthier lifestyle – oops. Dad somehow broke the audio on 2 TVs – one in his hospital room, one in rehab. I believe it was Mom showing up to get a word in.

The occupational therapist asking Dad to take off his shirt and he responded "What for? I barely know you!"

Dad introducing himself at the dining room table to 4 semi-functional ladies with "Hi I'm Sidney and I've been a damn fool" (they ignored him).

99-year old Ida's withering look when I asked if she was able to hike over to the rehab unit with me to visit Sid (she walks faster than me). Ida ranting about how she was mad at Sid for being a sloppy eater. He embarrasses her at special events because he doesn't tuck in his shirt. I informed her since my best friend just died from an exploding heart, and my smart, kind and somewhat messy father almost died a week later, I really didn't give a crap about etiquette. She apologized.

The nurse who stopped me in the parking lot to tell me the list of medications I provided was incredibly helpful because it not only listed Dad's drugs, but WHEN he took them throughout the day. It allows the staff to better calibrate his meds. Dad prepared the list on his computer 2 years ago; I found and updated it. We both get bonus points for good planning.

Sid: May 15, 2015

I have taken my shower at night before going to bed all my life. Last month I had taken my shower and was ready to dry myself when I slipped on the wet floor and fell back into the tub with my legs jammed under my body. My alarm button was on the shower chair five feet away beyond my reach. I wasn't able to lift my body out of the tub and started struggling to get one leg out of the tub. I was in a state of panic and ended on the bathroom floor with my face down on the floor. I screamed for help but there wasn't anybody awake and the walls were soundproof. I lacerated my knees and my chest while trying to get up. I also injured my face while I was in a state of sheer panic. The time was about ten o'clock.

I must have fallen asleep from exhaustion when I heard people moving around. I yelled for help and the cleaning lady responded. I asked for help in putting on a robe. My injuries were considered serious enough to warrant an ambulance and I was taken to Scripps Hospital. After three days in the hospital the doctor decided I should go to the intensive care unit in the assisted living environment. I spent three weeks in the special care unit before I could return to the independent living unit.

The rule for my discharge was I must take my showers in the morning with the aid of a nurse until I can be sure I can handle the job safely on my own. After a week, I am now on my own. The shower chair must be in the tub. So far, things are working out okay. The bills for my three days in the hospital came to $30,000. My insurance will cover all my expenses. It was good to return to my apartment. Fortunately, my injuries have healed well and I can resume a normal life again.

Karen: May 15, 2015: Life in Rehab

"Tried to make me go to rehab but I said, 'No, no, no . . ." My father has been recovering in the skilled nursing unit at his retirement village for 2 weeks, with 1 more week to go before being released back to his apartment. He is dealing with everything gracefully, and I'm spoiling him to soften the blow. I spend many hours distracting him. I smuggle in food every day to bribe the nursing staff and to keep Dad's spirits up: donuts, bagels, meatball sub. I'm holding back on the sugary treats because his doctor lectured us to focus on protein. Dad uses my laptop to watch Mel Brooks and Monty Python movies. I took it back to write this post and noticed the keyboard was full of greasy crumbs.

I'm getting lots of feedback from other patients I'm an amazing daughter when so many other kids never show up, which makes me sad. Sometimes the comments catch me off guard. Norm, my father's neighbor, who is dying from COPD and dementia, told me "You look sexy, can I grab a feel?" I declined his kind offer. I saw him later day and he told me "You look tired." I explained I excel at being both sexy and tired. He said he could relate. I held his hand. Yesterday was Staff Safari Day – the dress theme was jungle shirts and helmets. One hard-of-hearing lady misunderstood and thought it was Sephardic Day. That actually makes a lot more sense for a Jewish facility.

Sid is progressing; he gets constant physical and occupational therapy. Using a walker, he travels to his apartment each day to visit his comfortable recliner. We've rearranged the bathroom to be safer, incorporating his suggestions. Adjusting the height of the shower bench was no easy task; Mom used it for a decade and the legs were rusted into place. I realized Dad's toolbox, brought over from his old house and stashed away in the ancient file cabinet, would finally come in handy. I found the WD-40 oil and a ball peen hammer, and whacked away at the bench. Dad was impressed I was so handy. The supervising therapist was slightly scared, asking me "What exactly do you do?" I smiled and responded "Whatever is necessary."

Chapter 21

Coping with Change

Karen:

May 26, 2015: Big Daughter is Watching You

Sid is back in his apartment and making progress, there's a few humbling changes to his routine. No more late night showers when no one can hear him scream. He brags about how he's gone high tech with a computer glued to his wrist. Dad will comply with just about every suggestion as long as pizza is supplied. He's enjoying the attention of pretty girls who are helping him regain his independence. He became disillusioned when I explained Medicare doesn't cover aides to scrub his back or put lotion on his feet. "You told me that insurance pays for everything," he lamented. Well, almost everything.

I'm not a saint, I have periods of resentment. However being here is time well spent and an amazing learning experience. Friends occasionally show up to keep me balanced. Julie, my birthday twin who I've known since kindergarten, flew out from New York. Sid has always considered Julie an unofficial daughter, which is sweet. She stayed at my secret hideout: a wildlife farm where I tend chickens, Chihuahua dogs and rabbits.

July 15, 2015: An Earful

I'm in San Diego again for a whirlwind of doctor appointments, and we've have had some strange moments. I arrived to find Dad's hearing aid wailing in high pitch, then attempted to fix it. Cleaning, replacing the tubing, chatting with customer support and learning how to program the various modes made no difference. I asked him how long this noise had been going on. He had no idea but he did mention he was losing pals who couldn't stand the noise.

Although it drove me nuts, we went on with our errands and binge meals, even had time to hang out at the beach to watch the bikini-clad girls play volleyball. We saw the retina specialist, the dentist, the primary care doctor. Sid is recovering nicely from his fall and is trying to gain back enough balance to use his cane instead of a walker. After trying to navigate the local pub at happy hour, he realized that wasn't such a hot idea. All through these adventures the screeching continued.

I asked a nurse to clean his ears, since he tends to pile up wax and I thought maybe it would help. She stopped the procedure mid-stream, called in the geriatrician, who peered into his ear canal.

"Hey Sid. We're sending you to an ear nose and throat guy," the doctor proclaimed.

Then the doctor had me use the magnifying glass, which was flattering but I had no idea what to look for – maybe pickle remnants? We managed to get an appointment right away – the same day! – and sure enough, lodged inside Dad's ear canal was an old plastic plug that had separated from his hearing aid, complete with an inch of waxy crud. All I could think about was the alien movie where the insects crawl into people's ears and eat their brains. His device didn't work correctly because with a new plug it was unable to make contact past a barrier of debris. The ENT doc referred to it as the "yuck factor" in his field and said it was not uncommon.

Dad's hearing is much improved now. I've encouraged him to inspect his hearing aid each night to make sure it doesn't have more or less parts than the picture on the box. We ate dinner in blissful silence.

September 7, 2015: Happy Birthday #93

Despite Dad saying he didn't want to celebrate his 93rd birthday, I know better. He loves attention. So I took him to his favorite deli and he devoured cheesecake. I organized a spaghetti and meatball banquet for him and 6 lady friends, which our server referred to as his harem. This was followed by a surprise Brooklyn-themed egg cream* and babka dessert gathering. It was quite the event. Some of the ladies got stuck in the car due to my insistence they use seat belts. I tried to help Shirley up a curb and she informed me she still does triathlons, thank you very much. When Sid fell asleep after the singing I made everyone go home. That night his friend Harry fell out of bed and broke his leg. Such is the yin and yang of life in the retirement village.

December 5, 2015: Holiday Cheer

My father got a phone call a few days ago from "Anthony" who works at UC San Diego, inviting Sid to a holiday party on campus. The background: Sid volunteered for more than 20 years in the department where medical equipment was refurbished. He was a mentor to young electrical engineers, thoroughly enjoying tinkering, rescuing broken parts, and bringing back mystery items to his workshop at home. When my brother and I cleaned out my parents' house, we discovered surgical knives, prosthetic legs, and infusion pumps (a big hit at our garage sale). After my mother's health deteriorated 6 years ago and Dad could no longer drive, he couldn't continue the commitment; it sapped his spirit. He

137

fondly reminisces about this phase in his life; he assumed he was long forgotten.

Sid wasn't forgotten. Anthony and other staff at UCSD decided to do some detective work. His old phone number didn't forward. However they searched online and used public data, including my mother's death record, to locate him. Sid was so surprised by the call he didn't remember any specifics about the party, and said he wouldn't be able to attend. He then mentioned the call to me. Well I'm a pit bull and I set out to find Anthony; where there's a will (and the internet) there's a way. I connected with Anthony at the Biomedical Engineering Department. He told me Sid was one of their best volunteers; everyone missed his intelligence and sense of humor. They had not been able to track him down until now.

I'm not in town on the date of the event, and pondered how to get Dad transported. "No one remembers me anymore, I'm 93, they think I'm dead." Clearly they don't. Anthony is arranging for one of the other retirees to pick up Sid and drive him to the party, where he will be the guest of honor. Sid doesn't know it yet. I'll probably have to play up the free lunch angle to convince him it's worthwhile.

What a boost to remind me about the inherent goodness of some people in this world. At the party, the team toasted Sid with a rubber chicken, because he constantly complained about the rubber chicken meals he had to endure while working.

May 4, 2016: Trying a New Flavor

After my mother died 3 years ago, her 10-year old rickety blue walker was adopted by my father. His own balance deteriorated after a bad fall a year ago; he couldn't rely on a cane any longer. It was hard for him to accept he needed help, but he liked having a constant reminder of his wife. I've caught Dad talking to Mom a few times while wheeling down hallways, although she's been gone a while. I asked him if she ever answered; he smiled. "Sometimes she does." When the brakes stopped working and bolts starting falling out, he insisted we fix it, and the maintenance guys did their best. I periodically suggested a new walker to no avail – after all, why pay good money when this one was perfectly functional?

Last week was another round of doctor visits and shopping, it's our ongoing routine. I was shocked when Dad agreed safety prevailed and allowed me to purchase a new walker – as a "backup." Before he changed his mind I quickly bought one, ergonomically sound with two cup holders (one for coffee and one for beer.) It was even the same color blue. He insisted we leave his name tag on the old walker so Mom could still find him. He visited his favorite physical therapist, the one who worked with him for months after his accident, explaining he had a new Porsche needing adjustment. Afterwards he went to the onsite fitness center to ride the exercise bike for 45 minutes. He continues to build back his leg strength, and he's enjoying chair yoga three times a week. I successfully packed the new walker into the rental car (it folds flat! it's lighter and stronger!) and off we went for frozen yogurt to celebrate. Dad has eaten chocolate/vanilla swirl yogurt forever. I rarely ask which flavor because I always get the same response. This time I looked at him carefully.

"The usual, Dad?" He paused for a beat, looking back at me with bemused pride. "No" he responded. "Get me toffee crunch. It's time for something different."

Sid: March 1, 2017: Phone Message Transcript

"Hi Karen, I called to inform you of a minor tragedy. The black plastic cover did not exactly fit the plastic jar, and when I reached to remove the jar I was holding the plastic cover but it fell apart. I had pickles and pickle juice on the carpet. I tried rinsing the pickles but they lost their flavor. So that was the major part of our pickle juice, and we have to start all over again.

Otherwise, things have been very quiet here. I'm using the vaporizer and I'm breathing much better but the loss of pickles and pickle juice is a major, major tragedy. Anyway, that's the way it is."

Karen:

March 5, 2017: Multi-Tasking

Accomplished during my week visiting Dad:

Spent 4 hours preparing Dad's taxes with AARP volunteers, wearing them out.
Negotiated with deli manager for a new supply of pickle brine after spillage incident.
Replaced ruined pickles with organic sour dills from farmer's market.
Shopped for frozen TV dinners to replace ones ruined by 15-hour power outage.

Submitted paperwork to request move to assisted living unit, including scary forms about death.

Toured potential apartments late at night to make sure staff were happy with their jobs.

Purchased and assembled shower transfer bench to make bathing less risky.

Obtained new hearing aids and eyeglasses from Costco, cost of $2000.

Bought Costco hot dogs costing $1.50 each, such a deal.

Took Dad to barber.

Took Dad to doctor.

Shared tacos, beer and ice cream with Dad, diet be damned.

Shopped for new underwear so Dad doesn't have to do as much laundry.

Did Dad's laundry – twice.

Interviewed an entourage of nurses, physical & occupational therapists.

Researched home care agencies about private duty caretaker services.

Attempted a medication review, trying to match prescriptions to pill box mysteries.

Had "the talk" with Dad about needing a higher level of care in the near future.

Got heartbroken that he understands and agrees.

Met with bank manager to consolidate 14 stock funds purchased 30 years ago – referred to as "peanuts" by Dad.

Delivered boxes of peanuts to the bank manager to make Dad laugh.

Realized the peanuts fund will be depleted by uninsured long term care and future rent.

Went for a back country drive, not bothered when Dad slept through most of the scenery.

Felt humbled by the many caring providers and friends who watch over my father.

I think I need a patient advocate. Oh wait, I am one!

Chapter 22

Showers are Dangerous, Part II

Karen:

April 27, 2017: Déjà Vu

Almost 2 years to the date of his last fall, Dad slipped in the bathroom again: same kind of fall, same hospital. This was his 3rd strike; a new chapter has begun. After a few weeks in skilled nursing, he will be located in an assisted living studio with onsite caregiver support.

I was prepared. I was at his home for the first bad fall in 2013 when he crashed through a glass shower door. I missed the 2nd fall in 2015, a backflip where he laid on the floor for 14 hours before being discovered. This time I was nearby. The evening before, he tried an electric mobility scooter for a sunset drive around the courtyard. I wanted to ensure he could navigate it to the dining room for breakfast. I woke up early, sensing something was wrong. I got to his room 20 minutes after he fell and alerted the EMTs. Tip: don't try to lift an injured person unless you are trained, call 911. Even though we've had many talks about pushing the panic button, and he could easily reach 2 alert devices, he didn't use either system. He struggled to raise his body because he wanted to prove he was independent. He didn't realize until later he'd fractured 3 ribs.

My father is a tough guy who has survived a lot of trauma. I expect him to rally. His attitude is upbeat despite intense pain. Nurses, doctors, physical therapists and cleaning staff have been wonderful. Sometimes they ask if I'm his wife, then I have to explain he's my daddy, not my sugar daddy. I'm using pickles as motivation to get him to exercise his lungs to prevent pneumonia. After decades of self-management, he agreed to a palliative consultation to discuss his priorities and goals. Do I wish I had done more to prevent yet another crisis? Of course. To respect a person's dignity while keeping them safe is quite a challenge.

I'm now packing up Dad's stuff since he's going to downsize again. Boxes I grabbed from Costco are labelled "fully cooked bacon" which makes me giggle. It's much easier than the last round. Emptying a one-bedroom apartment is faster than dealing with a giant house. I am excited to finally get rid of the crusty plaid sleeper sofa, circa 1972. After calling a bunch of donation centers to find nobody wants a vintage eyesore, I found a guy with a truck who said he can make it disappear if I don't ask any questions.

I'm fine. Friends are helping me cope, this community is supportive. Last night I ate barbecued ribs - appropriate to recognize Dad's latest mishap.

Sid: July 15, 2017

Much has happened since the last entry. I was living in the independent living building for almost four years. I had a beautiful two room apartment. The bathroom was small but it was adequate for my needs. In April I had taken a shower and was outside the shower drying myself. I was standing on the floor wearing my slippers when the slippers actually slipped on the floor and I fell sideways onto the shower ledge. The curtain absorbed the upper part of my body but my lower part fell onto the ridge that kept the water from wetting the floor. I felt a sharp pain in my ribs and was taken to the hospital. Their tests showed I had broken three ribs. I stayed one week at the hospital and then was moved to the rehab unit in another building. I spent two months in rehab. Meanwhile, my doctor consulted with the facility manager and decided I was no longer qualified as independent and must move into the assisted living area.

Karen was very effective in setting up my new apartment. She managed to fit all my necessary needs from my old apartment into the new location. She is good at space planning.

Karen's comment:

At this point the facility staff told me Sid was depressed, his demeanor sometimes grumpy. I saw that side of him in an earlier phase when he was Mom's caregiver. I was relieved he put on his happy face when I was with him. I found a baseball cap with a "Grumpy" logo and Sid delighted in wearing it. After he died I gave the cap to Robert, his favorite waiter at a local diner who always gave him extra bacon.

Karen:

May 22, 2017: "Alexa! What is the Next Chapter?"

Assisted living is like a college dorm, with minimal furniture, lots of shelves, and authority figures popping up to make sure there are no drugs on site. I invited Dad's former dinner mates from the independent living area for a welcome party. All their walkers were crammed in; everyone ate sugar-free candy and reminisced about the good times when they could actually hear each other. They shared their Hebrew biblical names from childhood, and even invented one for Shirley, the lone Lutheran. It was such a privilege to see elders enjoying this kind of camaraderie. My Hebrew name is Haya, which I've known all my life but never researched the origin. It means "vivid, impulsive, instinctive, needs freedom and space with an unconventional personality." Clearly your name determines your path.

I purchased an Amazon Echo to give Dad some company and voice-activated resources. He was horrified at first, accusing me of dragging him into a future for which he wasn't ready. Then he realized he helped pioneer the technology decades ago when working as a telecommunications engineer. Two days later he's questioning Alexa about many topics, only he usually calls her "Electra." It's exactly like the spoof recently televised on *Saturday Night Live*.

Sid's broken ribs are slowly healing while he's adjusting to a safer environment. He's appreciative of the additional support and changes to his routine. However the most amazing accomplishment happened today, when Dad agreed to get a manicure. For decades he's been using a Dremel rotary grinder to trim his nails, which is like flossing teeth with a machete. Afterwards, I hid his prehistoric tool on a really high ledge. I know I

146

should throw it out, but it's just so horrifying it deserves posterity.

July 18, 2017: The New Normal

For the first period in 3 years, I've got time on my hands. Sid is doing well in assisted living. He enjoys the special attention, the environment is safe, his drugs are taken on schedule. The residential upgrade has relieved me of constant micromanagement and it's worth every penny. We may have solved the hearing aid issue (they fall out when he chews) with custom ear molds supplied by a thoughtful audiologist. Since walking has declined, we use a travel wheelchair to go out for non-approved meals (lots of salt) and occasionally share a glass of light beer.

And me? I'm working on my tan at the beach. I'm happy my father has a wonderful last chapter. Yesterday I walked into his apartment to find him writing it. He hadn't touched his keyboard in a while; his arthritic fingers type slowly with lots of errors. His language is objectively practical in his assessment of his current physical condition. Yet Dad's spirit is intact, and he's a kinder and gentler person. So am I.

September 4, 2017: 95 Years Strong

If anyone had told me a decade ago I would be taking my father on a scenic helicopter flight for his 95th birthday, I would have been skeptical. That's exactly what we did, and it was wonderful. Sid's zest, humor and appetite are in fine shape. His ability to keep hearing aids inside his ears, not so much.

I flew into San Diego to coordinate with cousin Marian, this time arriving from San Francisco, for 4 days of micro-planned festivities. The original plan was to use a friend's backyard and have a barbeque. A sizzling heat wave intervened; we adapted and had a pre-cooked meal in the living room instead. I provided shuttle services with my rental car while all the seniors' walkers were transported via antique truck. Marian was our balance consultant, using her physical therapy expertise to ensure everyone's safety. More than a dozen people came to the party, including Dad's former neighbors from Santee and Mike, his financial advisor from Chase Bank. The food was wonderful, prepared by AirBnB hosts who went way beyond the call of duty. The collective glucose level from all the non-approved non-kosher delicacies was dangerously high.

Dad said he doesn't like lots of attention (ha!), and was very fatigued, but he enjoyed every minute. And I got lots of hugs from little old ladies who are part of my extended family. Now if we can just find that damn hearing aid, which disappeared the morning of Dad's birthday. I suspect it was hidden by my mother, now gone 4 years. Mom wasn't able to attend the party, and she was sulking. In the life and death continuum, some things simply defy logic.

Chapter 23

Strokes Are Worse

Karen:

October 16, 2017: Leftie Power

After breakfast 2 days ago, my father suddenly lost his ability to walk, was breathing rapidly, and looked odd to a sharp-eyed aide at his facility. One hour later I was alerted by phone Dad was on the way to the Scripps Hospital ER. Then things got weirder.

Despite being within the 3 hour window to receive TPA, a clot buster drug that reverses damage, Dad refused treatment due to potential side effects such as brain bleed. A neurologist called to ask if I wanted to overrule his decision since I had healthcare proxy privileges. We agreed despite his age and condition, he was mentally competent, so I respected his choice. That was hard - if it were me I would have taken the drug. He was stabilized and I felt comfortable taking a flight later in the day.

I talked to my father at 6 pm and noticed a slight vocal slur. Arriving at 11 pm, I was greeted by a full code alert with a medical team rushing in to treat what they thought was a second, potentially fatal stroke. His words were garbled nonsense; all systems were failing. I slept in his room and watched the team in action, while convincing Dad not to rip out his catheter. After more CT scans, MRIs and cognitive testing throughout the night, they determined it was temporary brain swelling which would resolve. It did. By 8 am Sid was ready for a meal, talking a blue streak, wondering why everyone looked so concerned. However, his right leg was paralyzed from the knee down. I started planning for wheelchairs.

Fast forward to this morning, 48 hours post-stroke. I found Dad raising and lowering his leg, wiggling his toes, saying "Look, everything works again!" Huh? Well his body doesn't quite function like it should, but he made incredible progress. The man is a 95-year old diabetic with cardiac, orthopedic and pulmonary issues. What happened?

Sid is stubborn, he's a survivor, and he was born a leftie. As a child his knuckles were whacked and he was forced to write with his right hand. In his age cohort this was a common practice to "fix" a defect. He became ambidextrous; his brain practiced "neural plasticity" for decades to follow. I know left-handed people, about 13% of the population, are over-represented among musicians, creative types, and chess players. I was surprised to learn lefties recover from stroke damage faster and better. And lefties trained to be righties may have special brain powers no one understands. I'm a leftie, by the way - feeling pretty good about that right now.

I knew Sid was back on track when I got a call from the speech therapist this afternoon. I was at Costco chasing down lost hearing aid parts. Dad made her reach me to request a hot dog delivery, extra sauerkraut. She had to whisper as it obviously didn't meet nutritional criteria. He got extra insulin and a wink from the nursing supervisor.

Dad will soon be discharged to spend time in the rehab unit at his community; he's been there 2 times already for recovery from falls. His friends are across the courtyard, he will be welcomed back to a caring environment, and he may even get a private room (flowers over the years for staff has paid off). I ordered bacon for his breakfast, since he'll soon be returning to a kosher cocoon.

May 20, 2018: VIP Treatment

It was National Health Care Worker Week, and Sid decided to test the system. I flew in from Seattle, arriving to set up a spaghetti lunch in the hallway, per our usual routine. He got up from his recliner, lost his balance and went down on the floor head first. I heard the clunk. I was calm, he was mellow, we commented about how men swoon in my presence. The aides appeared, the paramedics arrived. I figured his time was up. This was going to be the final chapter – broken bones, stroke, coma, find the organ donor form. Real time advocacy. I followed the ambulance to the Emergency Room – again. I know the way.

I forgot my father has nine lives just like a cat; I've personally saved three of them. I think this was episode #5. Scripps Hospital gives him frequent user perks. The CT scan, x-rays, and lab panels were all done quickly. He was discharged in a few hours. Nothing was wrong except a urinary tract infection, common in the elderly (which might explain why he's wobbly).

> Me to Dad: "Have you noticed any pain when you pee?"
> Dad to me: "Oh that? Sure. I don't bother mentioning these things, I'm just happy to get a shower."

I won't pretend all is fine; Dad scared the crap out of me. Along with his issues I've been juggling clients with all sorts of medical crises and bills. I'm regularly on hold with insurance companies and mostly bang my head in frustration. But - apparently I have a thick skull just like Dad. He bounces back from trauma, I create billable hours from it.

While chowing down his grilled shrimp and bacon salad today (justified since lettuce is healthy), a nurse commented on his VIP treatment. Dad beamed: "Yes. I'm a VIP when my daughter is here. I'm a Vogel in Paradise." How's that for validation?

June 24, 2018: Hiding in Room 347

Dad has been struggling with respiratory fatigue, coughing so violently his nose was constantly bleeding. Paramedics were called and sent away. His caretakers thought he was about to have a heart attack, either from gasping or from exertion related to constipation (he yells loudly when he's on the toilet). I visited last week to find him struggling with globs of mucus caught in his throat and panic attacks. We went to his doctor twice. Drugs didn't work and he threw them up anyway. He didn't have pneumonia or a fever, maybe he had another stroke, it was all guesswork. He couldn't breathe without continuous oxygen but in order to get it prescribed he had to demonstrate he was about to die without it. Setting up tank delivery was a nightmare. He cried when I left town and it broke my heart.

Three days later Dad was taken to the ER. Specialists took many x-rays, removed some goo and sent him back home. He kept insisting if they used the right tool, he would be fine. Things got worse. After another doctor visit he went straight into the hospital. It happened to be my birthday and all I could think of was how my mother's sister died on her birthday, which traumatized her for decades. So, like any rational person, I called my dead mother on the old rotary phone I keep in my house as vintage decor. I asked her to not take him yet, and although there was no obvious response I think she heard me.

I flew back today to find Dad looking much better after his "tune up." He was holding a long vacuum suction tube a respiratory therapist had dug up from the supply room.

"It did the trick" he beamed, "Can I go home now?"

He was correct; he just needed the right tool. He was discharged in time for dinner with his buddies. Official diagnosis: acute bronchitis and lung infection. He also happens to have chronic obstructive pulmonary disease, cardiac failure, asthma, diabetes, dysphagia (inability to swallow properly), prostate impairment and a touch of anemia. He was given a choice – change his diet, get rehab therapy and live a while longer, or do whatever the heck he wants and take the nearest exit. He chose to live, at least for this round.

Meanwhile, I showed up assuming Dad would be hospitalized for a while and I'd be using his bed. There is no lodging in this town on a busy summer night. I figured I'd be camping in the hallway or laundry room with my emergency cot. However, I convinced the security guard to let me squat in an empty apartment downstairs. The resident just died and it's being prepped for the next tenant. It's clean and peaceful, there are no mystery stains. I walked to the nearest bar, had 2 cocktails, then quietly sneaked back in. Is this the circle of life? My father is happy I'm here. I'm exhausted. I'm leaving soon unless I start paying rent for my own early admission.

Chapter 24

The Last Chapter

Sid: May 30, 2018

Dad's last entry, captured on iPhone video by Karen:

> "I thought when your mother died that my life was over. I wanted to die with her. But I was able to start a new life, a different life. Now I'm falling apart. I'm not sure how to manage this aging body. But I know what your mother would have said. She would have told me to stop feeling sorry for myself, make the best of it, carry on. And so I will."

Karen:

August 16, 2018: Transition

I recently lost a good friend who happened to be my father. Dad died three weeks ago. His death was dignified and as peaceful as possible in a stressful situation. After a series of hospital visits and strokes, Sid understood there were no repairs available – no more engineering workarounds. When he could no longer eat junk food (or anything other than pureed mush) we both knew his time was up. He was briefly on palliative status, then hospice care; four days later he exited with me by his side. His friends Jack and Linda were also present. Sid's son Dan and grandson Brad had visited him two weeks earlier; along with daughter-in-law Robin they all called to say goodbye. It was a privilege for me to witness his last breath.

Dad always wanted to go to happy hour every Thursday, leaving his apartment at 3:30 PM so he could snag a good seat. He died at 3:30 PM on Thursday July 26, looking for a good seat wherever he was traveling next. I've been reflecting on the legacy my father left me. What I treasure most are the stories – his way of framing history, his ability to find humor in situations that were traumatic, his keen intellect and grasp of detail. Like many baby boomers, I didn't really know my parents as people. I went to college 500 miles away, created my own path, and monitored them from afar. My mother's death in 2013 was a chaotic blur, handled badly by a fragmented healthcare system. It was an emotional roller coaster for my father which almost killed him. At that point I had a choice to make. I took Dad outside to look at the full moon and told him,

> "You're not done. This will be a new adventure for both of us, we'll figure it out."

I will never forget how he looked at me with pure trust.

Lots of people have told me what a good daughter I am, which is true. It was also hard work that created much anxiety. I was constantly worried about Dad's safety. I called my father every day at 4 PM for the past 5 years, no matter where I was located. Often he left me funny phone messages, usually ending with "I had a good day."

I organized a celebration of Sid's life at his retirement home, exactly one week after he died, leading into the best happy hour ever with everyone devouring giant pickles. Going forward, there will be a Sid Vogel Pickle Day every Sept 2, his birthday. He wanted to make it to age 96, however he was also concerned about what event I was going to plan – "No skydiving," he admonished me.

Mixed emotions are at play. I miss watching my father devour his non-kosher shrimp and bacon. I'm humbled by the sacrifices

155

he made and the challenges he overcame. I'm relieved he was mentally sharp until the end of his life. I'm astonished he lasted decades beyond his expected expiration date. I'm grateful friends were with me to make sure I wasn't alone. It's wonderful his geriatrician attempted to list "pickle-penia" (Latin for lack of pickles) as a secondary cause on the death certificate. A week after Sid's death, the doctor asked me to book an appointment at his office. He spent an hour (non-billable) with me discussing the challenges of caregiving, acknowledging my role and sharing his own thoughts.

August 30, 2018: Giving Back

Sid had a practical view about body parts. He approved of recycling all discarded items way before it was popular, based on sound engineering principles. He was hesitant to discuss this stance with fellow Jews as some of the folks at his dinner table had survived crematoriums. However, the ability to contribute to science was paramount. He made sure back at age 75 I knew to call the UCSD School of Medicine to cart him away when his time came. He carried a crumpled organ donation card in his wallet for the next 20 years. My mother's body was also donated when she died in 2013; since I wasn't onsite to check I hope her organs didn't wind up at the local Goodwill shop.

Even though Sid's only regular charitable contribution was $5 every month to the Public Broadcasting System (PBS), he was able to donate corneas and skin, which can usually be used from any human regardless of age or disease. I made that call to UCSD with the hospice nurse right after he died, and was proud to honor my father's wishes. I also doubled the monthly amount sent to PBS, it was overdue.

Obituary for Dad

Sidney Vogel, 9/2/1922 – 7/26/2018

Sidney Vogel was born in Brooklyn, New York, a child of the Depression Era living in a railroad flat tenement. He was the youngest of 5 kids, skinny and insightful, learning just as much from people as he did from books. His father died when he was 19, disrupting his college plans and making him the breadwinner of the family. He supported his mother as a delivery boy and shipping clerk. Eventually he became a phone installer and cable runner, matching wires despite being color blind. In 1943 he joined the Army for 3 years, serving in the Signal Corps based in the Philippines.

Sid trained through an advanced electrical engineering program and managed communication installations. This led to a 40-year career at Western Electric/Bell Communications/AT&T, analyzing phone transmission systems, wiring boards, solid state electronic devices and integrated circuit chips, all precursors of modern computer technology.

Sid met Doris, an elementary school teacher, when he was 24. He was on his only vacation, in New Hampshire, where Jewish folks from the city went to escape summer allergy pollens. After a 2 week courtship he convinced "Dottie" to marry him in March 1947. She convinced him to finish his college degree, which he completed at night school at Brooklyn Polytechnic Institute (now part of NYU). Their dynamic and loving partnership lasted 66 years. Living in the Long Island suburbs, the Vogels had 2 children, many cats, a few rabbits, and a lot of telephones.

Sid and Doris relocated to eastern San Diego after retirement, where they supported local community theatre and enjoyed beautiful California. He was an enthusiastic fan of all kinds of music, Scientific American magazine and movies, especially Mel Brooks and Monty Python. He was a valued volunteer at the UCSD Biomedical Engineering Department, training staff, refurbishing parts and filling his home garage with broken hospital devices that "had potential."

Sid started typing his autobiography at age 73, later sharing his stories with his family so they could appreciate his past. He evolved to a laptop and wrote detailed updates through 2017. He experienced an amazing personal, technological and historic journey for close to 96 years.

Sid guided Doris through a difficult phase as her health declined. When she died in 2013, despite his own medical issues he courageously downsized upon his move to Seacrest Retirement Village. He made new friends and enjoyed his independence. After every dinner he declared to his tablemates: "Good night, good health and good fortune to you all."

Sid lived and loved to eat, especially pickles. He endured heart disease, diabetes, arthritis, lung ailments and broken ribs, but a series of strokes left him unable to adequately swallow or digest food in the last weeks of his life. It was a sudden and ironic fate. To his final day he was funny, gracious and appreciative of others. He passed surrounded by friends and beloved neighbors, holding his daughter Karen's hand, listening to the song "Always Look on the Bright Side of Life." In addition to Karen, Sid is survived by his son Dan, daughter-in-law Robin and grandson Brad and wife Lauren. He will be cherished and missed by his family, his companions and the wonderful people at Seacrest.

Family Tree for Sidney Vogel

The Vogel family tree was hand-documented by Sid in the 1980s. Using his recollections and documents I have attempted to update the scribbled charts. Like all genealogy projects, there are holes and the information may not be completely accurate. If you have more detail or corrections, please contact me.

There are 3 charts. The first one is for the Vogel patriarchal family, going back to Jacob Vogel, my great grandfather. The second one details the matriarchal branch on my mother's side, the Reger family. The third one traces the lineage of Sid's mother's family, back to my other great grandfather, Chiel Mandel.

Vogel Family Tree – Vogel branch

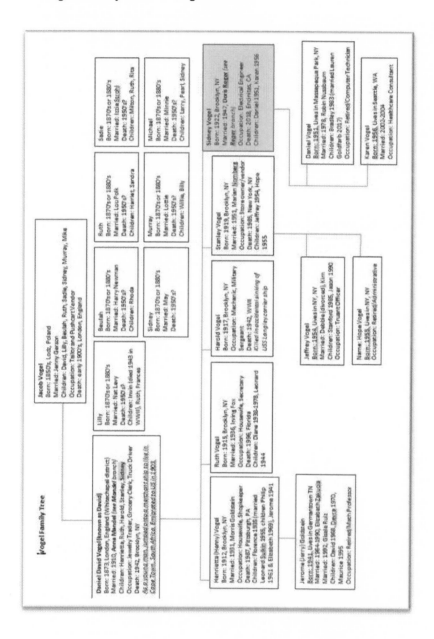

Vogel Family Tree

Jacob Vogel
Born: 1850's, Lodz, Poland
Married: Jenny Garon
Children: David, Lilly, Beulah, Ruth, Sadie, Sidney, Murray, Mike
Occupation: Tailor and Pushcart Vendor
Death: early 1900's, London, England

Daniel David Vogel (known as David)
Born: 1873, London, England (Whitechapel district)
Married: 1910, Anna Mandel (see Mandel branch)
Children: Henrietta, Ruth, Harold, Stanley, Sidney
Occupation: Jewelry Trader, Grocery Clerk, Truck Driver
Death: 1942, Brooklyn, NY
As a young man, jumped onboard merchant ship to Hawaii.
Cape Town, South Africa. Emigrated to US in 1903.

Sadie
Born: 1870's or 1880's
Married: Izzie Szcub
Death: 1950's?
Children: Milton, Ruth, Rita

Michael
Born: 1870's or 1880's
Married: Minnie
Death: 1950's?
Children: Larry, Pearl, Sidney

Ruth
Born: 1870's or 1880's
Married: Lou Folk
Death: 1950's?
Children: Harriet, Sandra

Murray
Born: 1870's or 1880's
Married: Lottie
Death: 1950's?
Children: Willie, Billy

Beulah
Born: 1870's or 1880's
Married: Harry Newman
Death: 1950's?
Children: Rhoda

Sidney
Born: 1870's or 1880's
Married: May
Death: 1950's?

Lilly
Born: 1870's or 1880's
Married: Nat Levy
Death: 1950's?
Children: Irwin (died 1943 in WWII), Ruth, Frances

Sidney Vogel
Born: 1922, Brooklyn, NY
Married: 1947, Doris Reizer (see Reizer branch)
Occupation: Electrical Engineer
Death: 2018, Encinitas, CA
Children: Daniel 1951, Karen 1956

Stanley Vogel
Born: 1919, Brooklyn, NY
Married: 1951, Marian Nomberg
Occupation: Store owner/vendor
Death: 1985, New York, NY
Children: Jeffrey 1954, Hope 1955

Daniel Vogel
Born: 1951, Lives in Massapequa Park, NY
Married: 1978, Robin Nussbaum
Children: Bradley 1983 (married Lauren Goldfarb 2017)
Occupation: Retired/Computer Technician

Karen Vogel
Born: 1956, Lives in Seattle, WA
Married: 2003-2004
Occupation: Healthcare Consultant

Harold Vogel
Born: 1917, Brooklyn, NY
Occupation: Mechanic, Military Sergeant
Death: 1942, WWII
Killed in accidental sinking of USS Langley/carrier ship

Jeffrey Vogel
Born: 1954, Lives in NY, NY
Married: Debbie (divorced), Kim
Children: Stanford 1985, Jason 1990
Occupation: Truant Officer

Name: Hope Vogel
Born: 1955, Lives in NY, NY
Occupation: Retired/Administrative

Ruth Vogel
Born: 1915, Brooklyn, NY
Married: 1936, Irving Fox
Occupation: Housewife, Secretary
Death: 1996, Florida
Children: Diane 1938-1978, Leonard 1944

Harrietta (Henny) Vogel
Born: 1912, Brooklyn, NY
Married: 1931, Morris Goldstein
Occupation: Housewife, Shopkeeper
Death: 1987, Pittsburgh, PA
Children: Florence 1936 (married Leonard Surkin 1955, children Philip 1961 & Elizabeth 1966), Jerome 1941

Jerome (Jerry) Goldstein
Born: 1941, Lives in Germantown TN
Married: 1964-1990, Elizabeth Zajucik
Married: 1992, Gisela Rulz
Children: David 1966, Dena 1970, Maurice 1995
Occupation: Retired/Math Professor

160

Vogel Family Tree - Reger branch

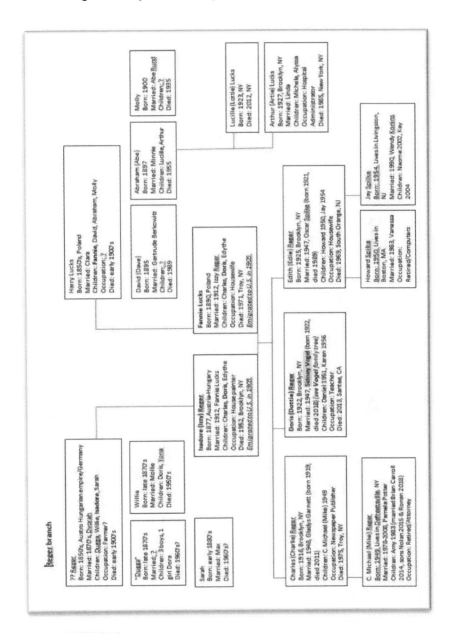

Vogel Family Tree - Mandel branch

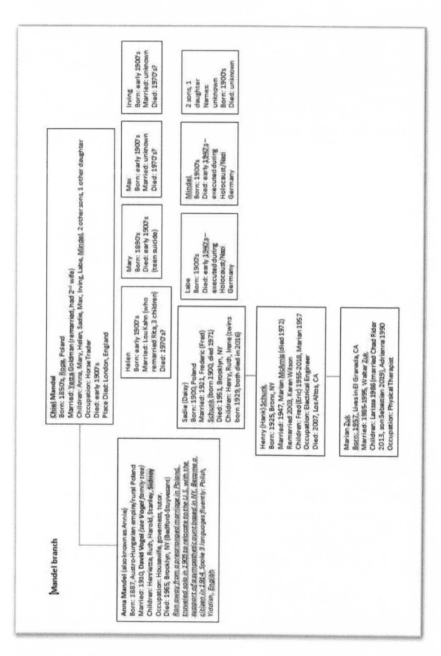

Mandel branch

Chiel Mandel
Born: 1850's, Bigaj, Poland
Married: Yetta Goldman (remarried, had 2nd wife)
Children: Anna, Mary, Helen, Sadie, Max, Irving, Labe, Mindel, 2 other sons, 1 other daughter
Occupation: Horse Trader
Died: early 1900's
Place Died: London, England

Anna Mandel (also known as Annie)
Born: 1887, Austro-Hungarian empire/rural Poland
Married: 1910, David Vogel (see Vogel family tree)
Children: Henrietta, Ruth, Harold, Stanley, Sidney
Occupation: Housewife, governess, tutor.
Died: 1965, Brooklyn, NY (Bedford-Stuyvesant)
Ran away from a prearranged marriage in Poland, traveled solo in 1905 to relocate to the U.S. with the support of a sympathetic aunt based in NY. Became a citizen in 1914. Spoke 3 languages fluently; Polish, Yiddish, English

Helen
Born: early 1900's
Married: Lou Kahn (who remarried Rita, 3 children)
Died: 1970's?

Mary
Born: 1890's
Died: early 1900's (teen suicide)

Max
Born: early 1900's
Married: unknown
Died: 1970's?

Irving
Born: early 1900's
Married: unknown
Died: 1970's?

Sadie (Daisy)
Born: 1900, Poland
Married: 1921, Frederic (Fred) Schunk (born 1900, died 1971)
Died: 1951, Brooklyn, NY
Children: Henry, Ruth, Irene (twins born 1929, both died in 2016)

Labe
Born: 1900s
Died: early 1940's – executed during Holocaust/Nazi Germany

Mindel
Born: 1900's
Died: early 1940's – executed during Holocaust/Nazi Germany

2 sons, 1 daughter
Names: unknown
Born: 1900's
Died: unknown

Henry (Hank) Schunk
Born: 1929, Bronx, NY
Married: 1947, Marian McKerns (died 1972)
Remarried 2003, Karen Wilson
Children: Fred (Eric) 1955-2018, Marian 1957
Occupation: Electrical Engineer
Died: 2007, Los Altos, CA

Marian Žuk
Born: 1957, Lives in El Granada, CA
Married: 1985-1995, Walter Žuk
Children: Larissa 1986 (married Chad Rider 2013, son Sebastian 2019), Adrianna 1990
Occupation: Physical Therapist

Advocacy Resources

Find a patient advocate: AdvoConnection Directory
www.advoconnection.com

Learn about health advocacy and consumer empowerment:
Washington State Health Advocacy Association *www.washaa.org*

How to select a doctor:
MedlinePlus
medlineplus.gov/choosingadoctororhealthcareservice.html
Choosing the Right Doctor for Your Medical Care
www.verywellhealth.com/choosing-the-right-doctor-for-your-medical-care-2615486

Find a geriatric physician: When It's Time to See a Geriatrician
www.aarp.org/health/conditions-treatments/info-2019/geriatrics-specialist.html
Find a geriatric care manager: Aging Life Care Association
www.aginglifecare.org

Physician certification, hospital affiliations, patient reviews:
Medicare Physician Compare
www.medicare.gov/physiciancompare
Healthgrades *www.healthgrades.com*

Driving autonomy: Taking the Car Keys: What to Do If an Elderly
Loved One Won't Stop Driving *www.agingcare.com/articles/taking-the-keys-if-mom-or-dad-wont-stop-driving-112307.htm*

Downsizing tips: Helping Senior Loved Ones With Downsizing
www.aplaceformom.com/blog/15-9-5-senior-downsizing-tips

Caregiving from afar: Getting Started With Long-Distance
Caregiving *www.nia.nih.gov/health/getting-started-long-distance-caregiving*

Transition to a retirement facility:
Independent Living for Seniors - Choosing a Retirement Home or
Retirement Community *www.helpguide.org/articles/senior-housing/independent-living-for-seniors.htm*
Planning Ahead for Assisted Living
www.nextavenue.org/planning-ahead-assisted-living

Medicare assistance, enrollment support and counseling:
State Health Insurance Assistance Programs
www.shiptacenter.org

Hospice and Palliative Care planning: What Are Palliative Care
and Hospice Care? *www.nia.nih.gov/health/what-are-palliative-care-and-hospice-care*

**End-of-Life toolkits; State-specific Living Will and Advance
Directive forms**:
Aging with Dignity *www. agingwithdignity.org*
An Easy Online End of Life Planning Tool | Final RoadMap
www.finalroadmap.com

Acknowledgments

I appreciate so many people who helped me throughout this journey. Mostly, of course, my father. Sid was a mensch (a Yiddish term for a person of integrity and honor). I miss him every day, especially at 4 PM when I used to make my daily phone call.

Thank you to:

Doris Vogel, my mother. She taught me the beauty of reading, the value of pushing boundaries and how to laugh at life's surprises.

Dan Vogel, my brother. In the last decade we became comrades, which was a mutual reward.

Friends and colleagues, especially Jack and Linda Craig. They always showed up at the hardest of times with smiles on their faces.

Robert Yuhas, MD, Sid's geriatrician. His honesty, compassion and appreciation of decent deli exemplified true partnership.

Seacrest Retirement Village residents and staff. It is a unique community full of people who care for others with dedication, humor and respect.

My blog readers, who gave me courage and inspiration.

Australia, the best place on earth. It was perfect to write about Sidney in Sydney.

Apologies to anyone I might have offended, living or dead.

This book is dedicated to the memory of Sam Taff.

Made in the USA
Columbia, SC
21 July 2019